THE
Chief Medical Officer's
FINANCIAL PRIMER

The Vital Handbook for Physician Executives

By Lee Scheinbart, MD, CPE, FAAPL

American Association for
PHYSICIAN
LEADERSHIP

Published by **American Association for Physician Leadership, Inc.**
PO Box 96503 | BMB 97493 | Washington, DC 20090-6503

Website: www.physicianleaders.org

This publication is designed to provide general information and is sold with the understanding that neither the author nor the publisher is engaged in rendering legal, accounting, ethical, or clinical advice. If legal or other expert advice is required, the services of a competent professional person should be sought.

13   8 7 6 5 4 3 2 1

Copyedited, typeset, indexed, and printed in the United States of America

PUBLISHER
Nancy Collins

PRODUCTION MANAGER
Jennifer Weiss

DESIGN & LAYOUT
Carter Publishing Studio

COPYEDITOR
Patricia George

TABLE OF CONTENTS

ABOUT THE AUTHOR

Lee Scheinbart, MD, CPE, FAAPL, earned his BS in biology at the University of Michigan and his MD from Ohio State University. He completed his internal medicine residency and hematology/oncology fellowship at the University of Florida Shands Hospital.

Scheinbart practiced hematology/oncology with Melbourne Internal Medicine Associates (MIMA) and Health First (HF) for over 20 years. During that time, he served on the MIMA Board of Directors and the Hospice of HF Board of Directors. A founder of the William Childs Hospice House and former medical director for the HF Cancer Institute, he went on to serve as vice president for medical affairs and later the chief medical officer at HF Hospitals, a division within the HF Integrated Delivery Network.

Now semi-retired, Scheinbart serves as the chief health affairs officer and assistant professor of leadership development at the Burrell College of Osteopathic Medicine. He has a keen focus on physician leadership and its impact on organizational success. His writings and research have appeared in the *Healthcare Administration Leadership & Management Journal (HALM) and* the *Physician Leadership Journal (PLJ),* respectively. His writings also have appeared in several books dedicated to the chief medical officer, all of which have been published by AAPL.

When he is not writing, researching, or speaking at national forums, he is mentoring aspiring physician executives or advising medical students. He is also an advisor for several healthtech start-ups, one of which is a patient navigation, advocacy, and support platform for those with chronic illness. When not engaged in those activities, you will find him fly fishing in parts unknown, cut off from most human contact.

FOREWORD

THIS IS THE GUIDE EVERY CMO — new or veteran — needs right now. Lee Scheinbart successfully integrates the new tools, new opportunities, and new challenges with the history and tradition of the old to give us a clear eye to the future — a future physician leaders must shape today.

This "primer," as Dr. Scheinbart calls it, is important for many reasons.

First, we have entered the age of mobile and digital lifestyles, giving us new ways to create true home-centered care – preventive, interventional, and supportive. Think about what it can mean to shift the locus of care to the home: the ability to see that environment and assess a patient's true resources, the ability to give patients a new sense of being of agency, and the ability to structure interventions at the right time and right place for the right patient.

Second, as we enter the age of generative artificial intelligence, we have the opportunity to make these remarkable tools part of our medical team. The successful integration of AI, of course, requires more from physicians than it does software developers. A robot may be better able than we are to remember and catalogue markers of illness from our genomics, proteomics, and biomics, but after the tests are done, it is the physician who must answer the patient's question: "What does this mean, doctor?" Our teams of people will always be more important than our tools.

And third, Dr. Scheinbart asks us to challenge payment systems that continue to waylay innovation, frustrate doctors and patients alike, and create inequities of care. Sadly, even the electronic health record has become more of a billing and collection vehicle than a platform for integrated care.

What I hear throughout this book is a call to be creative, to be unafraid, and to lead based on our deepest values. Too often physicians are told not to take risks, not to rely on others, not to be creative, but, in fact, our patients and our society need us to do exactly those things.

I'm grateful to Dr. Scheinbart for helping us build a toolbox for clear-eyed optimism as we live our values and create the next great transformation in healthcare.

STEPHEN K. KLASKO, MD, MBA
Executive in Residence, General Catalyst
Former President and CEO of Thomas Jefferson University
    and Jefferson Health

PREFACE

"There are two things that stay with physicians
their entire career. The first is who is on call.
The second is how to split up all the money."

J.M., MD, PhD, MBA
CEO of a Multispecialty Medical Group

DR. M. SHARED THAT ADVICE with me 25 years ago, long before I became a chief medical officer (CMO) much less contemplated authoring a book specifically for CMOs about "how to split up all the money."

When I entered the physician executive role first as a traditional vice president of medical affairs (VPMA) then as a CMO, there was no onboarding manual for either role, nor were there job descriptions descriptive enough to truly encompass the role(s). When I asked peers about this nebulous role of CMO and the lack of guidance, I heard what would later become a common refrain throughout my explorations of the role: "If you've seen one CMO, you've seen one CMO."

As I travel the country speaking with CMOs, I am not confident in the validity of that refrain. I have noted a peculiar pattern: Most CMOs have a background in primary care — mostly emergency medicine or hospitalist/internal medicine, along with family medicine and OB/GYN. Rare is the specialist who turns to the life of a CMO.

I suggest there are many reasons for the draw from primary care. First, during some point in their careers, primary care physicians struggle to keep up with the demanding schedule (particularly emergency medicine) and want a change in work pattern.

Second, they tend to live on the pointy end of healthcare and breathe the visceral issues that face hospitals and health systems. In other words, they feel the demands of a fragmented system that requires so many multiple tasks to provide care. They also feel pressures and tensions between resource allocation and demand for services. The workload to close those gaps and to provide appropriate care take a toll on body and soul.

CMOs share a passion for working toward a better future for those who work around them. They have a sense of giving back and of supporting the front-line clinicians of all stripes in their hour(s) of need.

The really great CMOs work hard to bend their organization *toward a better design* in favor of patient care in parallel with fiduciary responsibilities. Akin to the description of level 5 leaders in Jim Collins' classic book *Good to Great*, these CMOs seek first to understand and then to confront the brutal facts.[1] Armed with knowledge, they engage in debate and dialogue and build robust systems to advance the organization.

Whether from the lens of an emergency room or a critical care unit, an outpatient clinic or payer algorithm, these leaders share a vision to elevate the experience of both the clinicians and the organization with a "yes and" mindset that favors neither one side nor the other.

The challenge for physicians who take on the role of CMO is nicely elucidated in Joseph Hlavin's 2019 instructive case report that sought a comprehensive review of published literature focused on the practice of a CMO. Hlavin concluded that "while the position is indispensable toward healthcare vitality, the CMO experience is incompletely understood" — at least as far as the literature goes.[2] Had I read that observation before accepting the CMO role, I might have strongly re-considered the job.

Hlavin further suggests that a comprehensive understanding of the work of the CMO is lacking. In fact, until recently, no single book on the market established the basic aspects of being, or becoming, a successful CMO.

Fortunately, several practitioners came together under the insightful leadership of Mark Olszyk, MD, MBA, CPE, to tackle this sin of omission. The result is *The Chief Medical Officer's Essential Guidebook* (AAPL, 2023), a comprehensive guidebook for CMOs that answers the questions: What is a CMO? Why be a CMO? What is involved with being a CMO?[3]

This book is neither an extension of Olszyk's work nor a substitute. Rather, it is an attempt to help aspiring physician executives become better leaders by confronting the brutal facts and addressing how healthcare dollars are being allocated.

DEFINING LEADERSHIP

Twenty-five years ago, when Dr. M. (who would later become my mentor as well as friend) was interviewing me for my first position as a practicing physician following a hematology/oncology fellowship, he asked me a question for which I had no earthly answer: "Do you know how you get paid?"

My dull stare and slowly shaking head prompted him to tell me in the next breath that the issue of "splitting up the money" would be with me (and all physicians) for the rest of my career.

Skeptical (and simultaneously ignorantly dismissive) as I was at that moment, I realize his words have never been truer. Repeatedly, his aphorism has rung true, even two and a half decades later.

To become an effective CMO, one has to be a leader; it is not a job for a follower. My favorite definition of leadership comes from another mentor and friend of mine, Retired U.S. Army Lt. General Mark Hertling, who says (italics are mine): "Leadership is the art of understanding motivations, influencing people and teams, and communicating purpose and direction to accomplish stated goals *while improving the organization*."[4]

A common pitfall of aspiring physician leaders is binding themselves too tightly to the physicians (e.g., medical group, medical staff, in-network provider) as the champion and advocate for their complaints and demands. In some extreme cases, the CMO can become so tethered to that perceived constituent that they are anchored in the wrong port in a storm.

While all CMOs must navigate the tension of being a physician (whether or not they are still seeing patients), of working with other physicians, and, most importantly, of advocating for patient care/safety/quality, they must also *support the organization*.

All chief executives, no matter the type of organization, share this one thing: They are responsible to their board of directors for bringing value to the organization. CMOs may not have that written into their job description, and it may not be explicit or overt in the daily workflow of meetings and initiatives, but bringing value is an inherent function of executive leadership.

In addition to the traditional responsibilities around quality, safety, and best practices, a CMO must lean into the value proposition to truly fulfill the responsibilities of a chief. And, to bring value, the CMO must have more than just a broad sense of the monetary forces at work in healthcare; they have to be conversant and agile in the boardroom when money is discussed.

UNDERSTANDING THE ENVIRONMENT

As I got to know Mark Hertling, who has more than a decade of physician leadership development to his credit, I discovered that he has since refined his definition of leadership, adding the following: "Leadership requires four things: the modeling of desired behaviors, the exhibition of required skills, the techniques used to inspire action, and an understanding of the environment."[5]

It is this last component, understanding the environment, that is the crux of this book.

The dollars in the U.S. healthcare system start at one place and travel many roads and through many checkpoints, reviews, and audits before arriving in the hands of the provider. All of those processes add expenses to all the stakeholders. The money gets split many ways from start to finish.

With an understanding of these events, you will have enough of an understanding of the healthcare environment and how the money is split up in healthcare to elevate your performance as both a CMO and as a leader. You will be equipped **to develop into** a senior executive, **to exhibit** a skill of financial acumen, and **to inspire action** for the sake of all stakeholders inside and outside of the C-suite.

This book details the history of how healthcare dollars have flowed over the past five decades up to and including the latest iteration of payments known as value-based care. It concludes with a discussion of the power of investors, venture capital, and private equity in healthcare today.

When you finish the book, you should have a sufficient **understanding of the environment** to function to the best of your ability in your role. This is not a substitute for earning an MBA or any other advanced credentials, especially if you want to know about finance, accounting, lending, and micro/macroeconomics; however, you will have enough insight on the topic of healthcare money that you will be comfortable leaning in and influencing (if necessary) the outcome of any discussion that threatens the organization or the patients you serve.

When we were in medical school, we were instructed on the four vital signs to help us establish the status of the patient: heart rate (H), respiratory rate (RR), temperature (T), and blood pressure (BP). When you step into the boardroom, take a moment to pause and read the vital signs. Know your environment. Create a status report in your mind's eye. Are people animated (elevated HR)? Are they talking fast (elevated RR)? Is anyone flushed or has taken off their jacket (elevated T)? Does it feel like someone is about to burst (elevated BP)? Remember the axiom: In any emergency, check your own pulse first. What are your own vital signs?

This book is vital to the health and well-being of today's CMO. As the 21st century of healthcare is much "more integrated, inter-professional, and technologically savvy than ever before, it is incumbent to remain vigilant to the requirements of leadership and the role of the physician executive."[2]

INTRODUCTION

Our Saviour's Golden Rule (Primer Final Prayer).

"Be you to others kind and true,
As you'd have others be to you.

And neither do nor say to men,
Whate'er you would not take again."

New England Primer, 1803

JUST AS THE NEW ENGLAND PRIMER was written and illustrated to educate the illiterate/subliterate European settlers in the alphabet and to provide a foundation for reading (and ultimately for prayer), this primer provides a very elementary instruction in finances for the CMO. The stories are true and either witnessed by me or told to me by someone who lived the story. The names have been changed to anonymize the participants. Elements of a chapter that are publicly reported stories or factual in nature are cited as references and appear in the reference section at the end of the book.

As physician executives, readers will be able to relate to each story by virtue of their medical background or by their path into modern healthcare and can return to any chapter at any time to refresh the learning. Each chapter ends with key lessons or take-aways ("pearls") and a set of critical questions to ask when you find yourself in similar or even unfamiliar circumstances.

Pretend, perhaps, that this is your *Washington Manual* rendering quick guidance on the physiology of medical money flow. Think about who is paying and for what, who stands to gain, who stands to lose. Imagine the patterns at work and seek to understand what position you must consider to be effective in your role.

Skeptics and critics may allege that the material included here is more than is required for the role of CMO, that today's healthcare financial issues are best handled by CFOs and business development managers. I respectfully disagree.

For years, CMOs were seen as liaisons or the bridges between the clinical world and the management team. This thinking is anti-quated, and the terms *liaisons* and *bridges* are somewhat pejorative.

Today's CMO is a legitimate executive whose mantel of leadership requires them to be in front of issues, not necessarily between them as some sort of U.N. peacekeeper. While the role continues to evolve, mature, and gain definition, the CMO is undoubtedly a leader and one who must develop a keen situational awareness of the flow of money in healthcare. This primer will prepare the CMO to see how the healthcare money is divided today in order to care for the organization.

CHAPTER 1

Fee-for-Service/Private Practice (Solo vs. Group)

"May the love for my art actuate me at all times; may neither avarice nor miserliness, nor thirst for glory or for a great reputation engage my mind."

Oath of Maimonides

"If you don't know where you are going, you will end of someplace else."

Yogi Berra

IN 1992, DR. HENRY "PUFF " BALLARD, age 76, was driven by his loving wife, Felicia, to an appointment with a well-respected neurologist, Dr W. "Bill" Nadeau, in search of an answer. The Ballards drove an hour from Lockport, New York, a small town on the Erie Canal, through the region's rich farmland, past the majestic Niagara Falls, and into the city streets of Buffalo, arriving at an unassuming office across from Buffalo General Hospital.

Henry had been a fourth-year medical student at the nearby University of Buffalo back in 1941, and all of the students that year were summarily inducted into the U.S. Army. After graduation, now-Dr. Ballard was placed into the Army Air Force as a flight surgeon. At the end of World War II, he returned to western upstate New York to set up as a general practitioner, where he practiced solo until his retirement in 1992, not long after he visited Dr. Nadeau.

Felicia, who essentially ran her husband's practice out of their home on Erie Street, had begun to suspect a problem with Henry's memory and wanted a professional opinion. Henry wanted no part of it. After many months of pleading, Felicia finally convinced Henry to go to Buffalo for a quick check up with Bill, his colleague from his days at UB.

1

After being subject to a long and tedious examination that consisted of many questions and tests of recall, Henry burst out in a moment of lucidity and said, "Damn it Bill! There are only two kinds of doctors in the world: cutters and thinkers! And we both know I'm a cutter and you're not, so let's stop all this horse shit right now. You better start thinking and think up a diagnosis before I lose my temper and walk outta here!"

Bill calmly responded, "Puff, I've known you for 50 years. We are both getting old. But I'm afraid you are losing your memory and you won't be cut out for doctoring, cutting, or thinking for that matter, much longer."

The next day, Dr. Henry Ballard calmly announced to his office team that he would be retiring before the end of the year.

For the entirety of their careers, Henry and Bill had each been paid a fee for each and every service they rendered. And like many healthcare providers today, Henry was terribly frustrated by the time he reached the second half of his career. By the time he died in 2002, he had delivered countless babies, tended to any number and type of farm injury, and comforted many as they died from pneumonia, strokes, and the complexities of old age. He was rich by the town's standards but was middle class at best when compared to the white-collar workers of the 1980s and '90s, especially those in New York City.

He was on call 24/7/365 for nearly 47 years and his house served as a medical office, a clinic, an infirmary during flu seasons, and eventually the site of the village's first hospital. He never heard of work–life balance. To Henry, his practice was his work and was simply life in small-town America.

AN HISTORICAL PERSPECTIVE

Until 1965 when Medicare was signed into law, life in a small agricultural town did not yield a lucrative professional practice. In fact, going back to the 1600s and 1700s in pre-Revolutionary days of our mostly agrarian economy, those who practiced medicine could easily be broken down into three specialties: midwives/womenfolk, bone setters, and chemists. Almost all home illnesses and childbirths were managed by women as an expectation of their role. No payments of any kind were rendered for those services.

The most common emergency in the wilderness was an injury related to farming, hunting, or trapping, and the only thing that anyone could do was set the bone until it healed, properly or not. Often this service was done by a tradesman or craftsman in the local settlement, and often not for renumeration, but, again, as an expectation.

And finally, there were those women and men — some indigenous ("medicine men"), some from the far East ("ancient Chinese secrets"), or just primitive dope peddlers — who concocted salves, potions, home remedies, and the like, for the unexplained illnesses of the age most often infections or organ dysfunctions. In those instances, depending on the local culture, payment was expected in exchange for the ointment or bottle. If payment was expected for any of the above services, it was primarily in trade goods, and rarely in coin.

It was not until the mid-to-late 1700s that medical schools began to produce educated physicians, which prompted local governments to require licenses (for which physicians were charged a fee or a tax) to allow those foreign or domestically trained professionals to conduct their work. It was then that physicians were considered tradesmen and could charge fees for their services without much social objection.

Therefore, fee-for-service in medicine has existed for perhaps 300 years and the principles largely unchanged during that time.

As for Dr. Nadeau's fee for his service rendered on that day in early 1992? It was waived as professional courtesy.

A REVIEW OF FEE-FOR-SERVICE

Before we begin to follow a dollar's journey in healthcare, it is important to briefly review fee-for-service. CMOs who do not know this simple construct will be humbled very quickly when they are navigating the tension between independent doctors in the community and the organization's strategic goals.

Few people, aside from medical historians, recall how fee-for-service began, and only a modest fraction (perhaps less than half) of today's practicing physicians receive a true fee for their service.

Overhead Costs

Most physicians today are paid via some type of "pass-through" mechanism (more on that later) rather than a direct payment from the hand of the patient to the purse of the physician. Just as our economy lurched forward and backward many times in our nation's history, so did the methods of billing and collecting. And along with each iteration came overhead — one of the most revered ledger items by all accountants in healthcare, whether they are office managers or the CFOs of billion-dollar systems.

Once physicians required some form of accounting for their services, they created overhead in the form of the ledger purchased to track revenues and expenses. This type of overhead was "indirect" — an expense related to the accounting of the money, not the actual practice of medicine. A direct expense might be a stethoscope (a fixed expense or one-time purchase) or gloves/needles/syringes (recurring and sometimes variable expenses).

And all these expenses — direct and indirect — reduce the amount of money that the physician takes home at the end of the day. The first dollar the physician receives for services is immediately reduced by one or more of those overhead expenses.

Supply and Demand

Doctors who expect to bring home money for food, gas, mortgage, and savings, must first determine how to translate their service into a fee. What is the fee for a particular service? Is it constant or variable? Likely to go up or go down?

In 2012, a brief opinion piece in *The Atlantic* stated, "This antiquated [fee-for-service] model is the culprit behind exponential health-care cost growth."[1] The pressure put on all healthcare providers (physicians, hospitals, clinics, etc.) originates from all of the payers (patients, insurers, and the government) who, since they are paying increasingly higher costs for services, want to see the costs go down.

Whenever Dr. Ballard saw a patient in his home office prior to 1965, he charged a fee, which for all intents and purposes was an arbitrary figure based on simple economics of supply and demand. A 1956 AMA poll found that 43% of patients thought their *doctor charged too much* — in 1956![2] This finding was likely also true in upstate New York, as the community had little say regarding physician fees.

In a brilliant 1963 essay, economist Kenneth Arrow states that "the need of medical services was not steady in origin...but irregular and unpredictable."[3] Thus, demand was truly variable (as preventative medicine was not yet widely practiced), and supply was limited based on the available number of highly selected, highly educated, licensed professionals who were capable of rendering a unique service at unpredictable times.

In practice, physicians were, therefore, positioned in a market to generate fees as much as the market would bear. In fact, some opinions, cartoons, and caricatures of the era suggested that physicians were more similar to plumbers than to scientists.[2]

Further, most physicians were opposed to the impending payment models that were being introduced by Medicare and early health indemnity insurance, as it was known. They were rightly concerned that *someone other than the patient paying for the service* would somehow change how much would be paid regardless of the fee on the invoice.

What happened next was quite remarkable and a topic that could easily take up a whole library; however, suffice to say that the physician lobbying arm, the American Medical Association, and the Centers for Medicare & Medicaid Services (CMS) agreed to pay physicians an amount based on a local, geographic calculation of a "customary, prevailing, and reasonable" fee.

However, doctors did not have to accept Medicare's fee as payment in full (i.e., "take assignment") for any individual patient. Physicians simply increased their fees, which ultimately elevated the customary and prevailing fees which CMS had agreed to pay and generated an upward spiral of professional pricing.

This legacy has plagued physicians ever since, because until another force (managed care, which we will address later) came along and pushed back on who actually was driving the amount of the physician fee, the law of supply and demand was forever altered. In an economic model whereby the supplier of the service is no longer directly paid (either in part or in whole) by the direct consumer of the demand, all bets are off regarding stability of the marketplace.

After 1965, "Puff" Ballard continued to charge the town folk a fee, and his fees eventually made it into the upstate New York geographic tabulations of "usual and customary" and, like so many of his colleagues, he ultimately agreed to accept the assignment of CMS payments for those enrolled on Medicare. To his surprise, he began to see more revenue than ever enter his practice. He was the lucky beneficiary of the new model.

The Question of Payment

As we wrap up this first chapter, let us return to Dr. M. and his probing question as to whether I knew how I would get paid. Immediately after he shared the two things that would be with me forever in my career (call and splitting money), he told me about "the formula."

In our group practice, I would be given a salary for which I would get a paycheck every two weeks. But fundamentally, I was only going to take home 50½ cents of every dollar I collected; the other 49½ cents would be devoted to the overhead (gauze, secretary salaries, stamps, utilities, rent, etc.) of the entire group. And, at the end of each quarter, if there was a surplus of cash (minus the 49.5% overhead allocation) over and above my paychecks, I would receive that surplus. AND, if there was any cash leftover in the bank after the group paid all of its overhead, each physician would receive an equal share of the group's surplus.

Further, all 120 doctors in our group would have the exact same formula, so we all contributed the same share on a percentage basis to the overhead. But different doctors' specialties allowed for different services (i.e., fees) so the incomes would be different and the absolute contribution to overhead could be higher or lower depending on the total number of fees collected.

Needless to say, this caused an endless amount of tension within the group, especially between lower-earning physicians (e.g., pediatricians) and higher earning ones (e.g., cardiologists). However, this formula was the glue that kept the group together for over 50 years. The management focused on ways to increase professional fees, increase other revenue streams such as labs, imaging, and rehab services, or lower overhead, such as staffing, supplies, and transcription.

The inflection point for the group and why the group no longer exists came down to an inability to satisfy the desired incomes of the partners. There came a point when no amount of service volume or improvements in collections could make up for the declining fees (dictated by third parties, not patients) against the rising expenses of the overhead. The formula still worked, but at a detriment to the ultimate take-home pay of the physicians.

With each passing year, fewer and fewer physicians know how money flowed into a physician practice in the post-war economy. This is particularly true of today's physicians who are paid a salary, paid with a structure based on RVUs (again, more on that later), or under any number of novel structures.

Why does this matter? The emerging CMOs who were previously on a salary during their early clinical years may not have a good understanding of how their fellow physicians, especially the independent practitioners, are really earning their income. A leader must master the art of understanding motivations, and money tends to be a key motivator when dealing with humans.

LESSONS LEARNED

- Fees for services in healthcare began arbitrarily and were local to the economy of the region.
- While the flow of money to the physician depended on supply and demand, the buyer (i.e., patient) of the original fee-for-service model had no influence and was subject to supply and demand of the available service. Elective care and choice in

provider as we know it today did not exist. And, even today, the use of "elective" and "choice" nomenclature is perhaps misleading and still depends on supply, demand, and the buyer of the service — although the buyer ("insured") is now a third-party purchaser ("insurer").

- All physicians in business for themselves carry direct and indirect expenses, all of which can be described as overhead. This is information that medical education does not prepare physicians for, even though these expenses are the basic requirements of running a small business.
- There is no single, equitable formula for managing a practice, but the larger and more varied the practice environment, the more likely there will be different opinions about sharing/splitting up the money equitably.

QUESTIONS TO ASK

When you are confronted with members of the medical staff who stand in opposition to a new initiative, ask yourself the following questions:

- What motivates their opposition? What are they resistant to?
- Is the resistance related to a financial impact to their professional (i.e., personal) income?
- Is there a law of unintended consequence at work regarding the new initiative that would cause physicians to lose income? A classic example is asking independent physicians to reduce their length of stay, which will lessen the number of daily fees charged by that physician (i.e., loss of income), or asking salaried hospitalists to have more patients on their census without a commensurate raise in salary (i.e., devalued work effort).
- Is there a turf battle going on with the addition of a new service with "fees" going from one specialty to another? Incomes lost vs. incomes gained?
- If an inpatient service is moving to an ambulatory setting or vice versa, does it affect anyone's professional fees?

- What types of personal, professional overhead, or loss of fees could occur with a new initiative? For example, is creating a new ambulatory site of service rather than continuing under the hospital roof, encumbering physicians with more travel/mileage/gas (i.e., overhead) and/or reducing clinic time to travel (i.e., loss of clinic income) or less OR/endoscopy suite time under the new arrangement (loss of procedural fees)?

If you are the CMO of a managed care/commercial insurance company and are involved in contracting with physicians to provide care and services for your member beneficiaries, or if you are the CMO of a medical group, you can ask similar questions as those above. If you are a CMO in those roles, try to bend the question into your organizational arrangement to clarify your own surroundings. That theme will repeat itself throughout the book.

CHAPTER 2

Hospitals — Part 1

"A hospital bed is a parked taxi with the meter running."

Groucho Marx, as told by Brian Alexander in *The Hospital*

THREE YEARS AFTER HENRY BALLAD was born and 265 miles to the southeast, in the small coal mining town of Pittston, Pennsylvania, Jack Fischer was born to immigrant parents Louis and Fanny Fischer. Born in 1889 in Poland, Louis at the age of 20 emigrated to the United States during the flood of immigration. Louis was a skilled tailor who ran a successful shop in downtown Pittston until he retired; he lived well until he died at age 85. Jack and his mother were not so lucky, however, when it came to living healthy long lives.

Small mining towns in northeast Pennsylvania expanded rapidly during the second industrial revolution and, correspondingly, Louis' tailor shop was thriving along with the increasing population and commerce along the Susquehanna River valley in Luzerne and Wyoming counties.

To connect people across the cityscapes that were also rapidly expanding, and in light of the fact that few workers could yet afford an automobile, municipalities began to establish trolley and/or streetcar systems to move people around the cities and regional centers.

In 1905, a typhoid epidemic broke out in the river valley and the city hall in Nanticoke, just southwest of Pittston, served as a makeshift hospital for those infected. Four years later, on land donated by Susquehanna Coal Co., Nanticoke Hospital opened its doors to care for coal miners and their families. The hospital boasted 20 beds in the male ward, 10 beds in the female ward, and eight beds in the burn ward. It, too, had to expand rapidly in the early 1900s due to overcrowding as the region boomed.[1]

In the 1930s, the towns along the Susquehanna River valley began to convert the aging streetcars into trolley buses, and ultimately to regular buses for easier access, longer range transportation, and affordability.

In 1937, Louis's beloved wife, Fanny, was caught off guard while walking through downtown Nanticoke and was struck by an oncoming streetcar, one of last remaining in Luzerne County. Fanny suffered a major traumatic injury to her left leg and was taken immediately to Nanticoke Hospital.

After several weeks and several unsuccessful operations to mend her left acetabulum, left femur, and left tibia, she was released home in the care of her husband and confined to a wheelchair. She was no longer able to help Louis in the shop but slowly improved enough to continue with the accounting, invoices, and the tracking of sales. Fanny limped for the rest of her life but, needless to say, was ever grateful her life was spared.

In those days, hospitals billed patients much in the same way that Dr. Henry "Puff" Ballard did in upstate New York. The Fischers received a bill from Nanticoke Hospital for services rendered, for Fanny's room and board, and for basic supplies and staff care, as well as the wheelchair upon discharge. The hospital bill totaled $158.

Louis earned barely $600 per year, much less had any savings. He tried to obtain a bank loan to pay the hospital bill but, given his immigrant background, was flatly denied. So, he did the only thing left to him: He borrowed $150 from a loan shark.

When the local mob boss came around to collect, Louis had no available cash but struck a deal to provide 10 hand-tailored suits to the boss and his pals in lieu of repayment. Legend has it that the Northeast Pennsylvania mafia were instantly the most well-dressed men in the region and soon Louis had more orders from La Familia than he could ever have imagined, ensuring his lifelong prosperity (and protection).

THE BUSINESS OF HOSPITALS

Nanticoke Hospital had sent an itemized bill to the Fischer home that displayed charges for the use of the OR ($10/surgery), anesthetics ($4 each), laboratory exams ($2 each), drugs (various), x-rays

($1/each), dressings ($0.30/each), and room and board ($5/day) to name a few. The itemized charges, considered usual and customary, covered all of the direct costs for services rendered; indirect costs were more difficult to itemize and charge.

Unlike a private house call made by a physician, a hospital service involves many more layers of overhead expenses that could be itemized to the patient. These would have included staff salaries (nurses, orderlies, unit clerks, lab personnel, kitchen staff, janitorial staff, etc.) which basically were the costs of "room and board."

Accounting was less sophisticated and could not create a cost based on the amount of square feet that consumed a portion of plumbing, heating, cooling, etc., which were all costs to the hospital. But it could tangibly account for medications, dressings, x-ray film, and suture material, and create some type of profit margin to cover all of the other less visible material costs of running the hospital. At that time, it was quite acceptable for the hospital to charge what the local market would bear plus some amount of margin to keep the enterprise afloat.

Under these market conditions, hospitals were largely static in their business operations for about 35 years, and like any modest business, worked through boom and bust, supply and demand. Oftentimes, the resources to build hospitals were allocated from public support such as land donation and taxpayer support, from philanthropy, or from private support. For example, the Susquehanna Coal Company donated three acres for Nanticoke Hospital.

So, at a time when physicians and hospitals generated revenue in largely the same fashion, as payments for specific services that could be accounted for in a very simplistic manner, there was little incentive to delve deeper into any other financial structures. The mistrust that we see between these two entities nowadays was minimally present, subdued, or largely ignored.

HERALDING A DRAMATIC CHANGE

So, what exactly happened to alter the medical payment system so dramatically that it is barely decipherable by even the most astute clinicians today? The answer is found in the parallel evolution of health insurance.

Health insurance as we know it today was the idea of a former school superintendent turned hospital administrator by the name of Justin Kimball.[2] The idea was a strategic initiative borne as a result of declining revenues at Baylor University Hospital in Dallas, Texas, in 1929.

Kimball, who 10 years earlier as a superintendent of schools in Dallas had established a sick benefit for Dallas teachers, was hired at Baylor University Hospital to provide oversight of the university's medical education and to "shore up the shaky finances of University Hospital."[3] With occupancy rates falling and patients unable to pay their own bills, Kimball set out to establish a plan that would help hospital patients pay their bills and keep the hospital alive.[3]

At about the same time that Kimball was tasked to help the hospital in Dallas, Nanticoke Hospital was expanding, given the boom in mining and the second industrial revolution. However, in 1929, the United States suffered a stock market crash followed shortly thereafter by the Great Depression.

Local hospitals were affected by the Depression just like any other business that relied on revenue to survive. As workers lost jobs and daily wages, hospitals lost a significant amount of revenue. Babies were still being born and all manner of accidents, injuries, and illnesses still occurred, but fewer Americans had the means to pay their bills in full. Between 1929 and 1930, Baylor University Hospital saw its receipts drop from $236 to $59 per patient.[4] Occupancy rates dropped from 71.3% to 64.1%, and contributions were down by two-thirds while charity care, in contrast, was up 400%.[4]

Worried about the decline in patient payments, Kimball devised a means for people to pay for their hospital care. He enrolled 1,250 Dallas public school teachers into the Baylor Plan and for 50 cents a month, he promised to provide 21 days of care at Baylor University Hospital. Because of opposition by the AMA, the plan covered only the hospital fees, not physicians' services.[2]

At that time, the Baylor prepaid hospital plan was created to be distinct from traditional commercial insurance and as a nonprofit plan. One of its earliest brochures boasted that "Baylor uses no sales agency or middlemen, but prefers to deal directly with each group so that all group hospitalization fees paid may be used only for hospital care of members and not for any personal profit."[4]

The Texas Department of Insurance, in fact, determined that the Baylor plan was not in the business of providing insurance; instead, the department viewed the plan as a "group contract for the sale of services."[3]

THE ORIGIN OF HEALTH INSURANCE

Within five years, many more employee groups with thousands of members were covered by this new type of plan.[4] This was probably the first "narrow network" as it is commonly called today. It would later become known as the original Blue Cross hospital plan.

The model began to spread to other hospitals and other states, and by the 1940s "hospital service plans" were sanctioned, endorsed, and promoted by the American Hospital Association (AHA) and were in operation in many hospitals.[2] Thus, it was the hospital trade association (the AHA) that drove the beginning and subsequent growth of modern commercial health insurance.

At first, physicians supported the AMA position on hospital service plans (which was to flatly reject them), as they did not favor any intermediary between their invoices to patients and the means to collect, not to mention that since patients who were enrolled in such plans had their hospital expenses covered, it left more discretionary income for households to pay for the physician service fees.

Over the next two decades, however, especially with the advent of the Blue Shield plan out of California which *did* cover physician fees, the AMA and larger numbers of physicians pivoted and began to endorse a wider range of health plans to ensure adequate payments for their services.

Forces at Play

In parallel to both of these types of coverage plans, two additional forces aligned to give rise to the eventual enormous growth of health plans. The first was that during World War II, the U.S. government imposed wage freezes to control inflation, as employers might otherwise pilfer workers with promises of higher wages.[6] From both a productivity and cost perspective, that type of environment could hurt the war effort and lead to tremendous economic disruption in the following years with a return to hyperinflation.

The War Labor Board was created to manage this, but it exempted employer-sponsored health benefits from wage freezes to prevent labor groups from striking another potentially devastating impact on the war effort.[6] And as a classic example of the "law of unintended consequences," this exemption was the ammunition employers needed to recruit workers and mollify labor unions at the same time.

The second force was the fact that organized labor seized on this new "benefit" as a reason to unionize. Organized labor contributed to worker protection (and therefore industrial productivity) by supporting the growth and development of prepaid care (hence the origin of "managed care").

Together, employers and unions — and now healthcare providers — were advantaged by this exempted benefit and, given the immediacy of the war, few were able to see what the future would hold, so health plans grew almost unchecked. The money pie grew quickly.

To illustrate the point using one of the earliest structures, 2,000 Los Angeles Department of Water and Power workers and their families contracted with a local clinic to provide employees with comprehensive care with no additional cost to the employees for services rendered.[7] This benefitted the clinic to have a guaranteed source of revenue, but angered other local physicians who would not have access to these patients for care and fees for services rendered unless those patients had the means to go "out of the network" and pay privately, which they most certainly could not afford.

Closed Systems and Narrow Networks

This scenario was repeated in many locations with battle lines drawn between clinics, employers, physicians, medical societies, and hospitals. In fact, physicians involved in providing prepaid services to such labor/employer arrangements were barred from local medical societies and subsequently denied hospital privileges, as it was often a requirement of privileging to be a member in good standing at the county medical society.

This, by the way, was how the Kaiser Foundation began its march to employ its own physicians, build its own hospitals, and have its own health plan.[7] If you can't join them, then beat them at their own game, so to speak.

And, to make matters worse by adding to the exponential healthcare system growth, immediately after World War II, Congress passed the Hill-Burton Act, which provided federal grants to states for the construction of not-for-profit hospitals (more on that in Chapter 14).[8] Among the key requirements was that the newly constructed hospitals provide a "reasonable" amount of charity care for the communities they served.

Beyond that, the ability for hospitals to spring up across the United States was almost unfettered with the grant funding and when, in the 1960s, Medicare and Medicaid were born, reimbursement for services led to a perfect storm of explosive growth in the money moving into the U.S. healthcare system.

Navigating the System

While the Fischer family navigated Fanny's injuries, the cost of her care (paid in suits, mind you), and the economic challenges of the post-Depression era, Jack, the youngest of five, was sent to serve the Navy in the Pacific at the age of 22, going on to become a decorated Navy Corpsman (i.e., medic). He returned and settled in Kingston (just north of Pittston) in 1945, married, and worked uneventfully as an accountant in a furniture store for the next 30 years until a massive stroke at age 56.

He was taken immediately to Wilkes-Barre General Hospital for his treatment and care. He stayed several weeks and received as much rehabilitation as was possible for his residual hemiplegia, but was essentially fully disabled.

His hospital bill was expensive and his employer at the furniture store did not provide any type of health insurance. Jack's unmarried daughter moved back home to care for him, while Jack's wife, who worked at the furniture store managing payroll, took up some of her husband's duties to earn more income. Still, paying the bills would be a significant challenge.

Subsequently, Jack developed aspiration pneumonia and required another hospitalization, but was taken this time to the Veterans Administration (VA) hospital located on a mountain top opposite Wilkes-Barre General Hospital.

While at the VA hospital, all of Jack's expenses were covered from his Navy service benefit and, ultimately, the Fischer family was able to have the Wilkes-Barre General Hospital bills covered by his VA benefits.

Jack died later that year due to complications from repeated episodes of pneumonia, but if it were not for his service during World War II, his family would have likely been impoverished from the expenses of the care. Jack was fortunate that he received VA benefits compared to millions of Americans who at that time lacked some type of employer related health insurance and were too young to be eligible for Medicare.

In the next chapter we will explore the origin of Medicare and its impact on the financial operations of hospitals, but suffice to say that up until the mid-1960s, aside from the early days of Kaiser and the role of the VA as examples of closed systems/narrow networks, the majority of hospitals in the United States billed patients in a fee-for-service model, mostly based on cost as physicians did, and depended on payments to keep the facilities open and functioning.

LESSONS LEARNED

- Hospitals are intrinsically tied to the local economy; as the economies boom and bust, hospital finances are affected.
- A hospital administrator created a prepaid plan for a group of employees (teachers) as an employment benefit should they require hospitalization. It was the first type of indemnity insurance/health casualty insurance established to keep hospitals afloat financially.

- Hospitals were the first to endorse such employer/employee benefits, much of which converted into an early form of employer-sponsored health insurance.
- Hospitals have been intimately tied to and dependent upon sources of third-party payment (e.g., VA, labor/union benefits, etc.) other than patient household income for the past 100 years.
- Hospitals benefit from stable relationships with insurers, as the largest source of payment for services.
- The splitting up of money became a source of antagonism between hospitals and physicians 100 years ago; it is not a new problem.
- A leading cause of personal bankruptcy for decades has been the household expense of healthcare.
- One person's expense is another person's income.

QUESTIONS TO ASK

When you are considering new initiatives, ask yourself the following questions:

- Who benefits the most when a benefit is available? The patient or the provider? Who pays for the benefit? Whose responsibility is it?
- Who will pay the hospital — the patient or a third party (i.e., insurance carrier)? How many third parties pay the hospital?
- Who is responsible for setting the hospital/clinic charge?
- What influences the charge?
- What are the key drivers of overhead related to the charge? Are they direct (e.g., cost of material) or indirect (e.g., cost of housekeeping, utilities)?
- What happens when other expenses such as security, technology, or revenue collections rise? How is that managed? Is it through strategic revenue growth or expense management? Who is ultimately responsible for managing increasing costs? Does a CMO have responsibility for managing costs?
- What is a corporate allocation and who is responsible?

CHAPTER 3

Third-Party Payment

"Health is, for the most part, a commodity which
can be purchased. The difficulty now is that its cost
is beyond the reach of a great majority of people."

Matthew Sloan, President of New York Edison Company, 1929

IN 1972, HURRICANE AGNES SPREAD its devastation from the Gulf of Mexico all the way into the Lehigh and Wyoming Valleys of Northeast Pennsylvania. The costliest U.S. storm at the time (est. $2.1 billion, about the size of an entire medium health system today), the hurricane caused massive flooding of the Susquehanna River and destroyed Jack Fischer's home.

In 1975, Jack suffered a stroke and ultimately died, creating an earnings gap for the Fischer household that had a material impact on his widow, Kathryn, and two daughters.

Kathryn remained behind a desk at the furniture store until she was late into her 70s, as the impact of the storm depleted all of the equity in their home, along with all of their savings. Kathryn was forced to move in with her sister as she could not afford a rental.

With fewer and fewer opportunities for employment in the once-booming mining towns, one of Kathryn's daughters moved to Philadelphia; the other, Miriam, got married and moved to Akron, Ohio, where the economy was only slightly better.

The Great Lakes region had benefitted for years from the growth of the automobile industry, but by the 1970s was experiencing a downturn, not unlike the mining industries of Pennsylvania. Akron was spared slightly, however, since it hosted the three primary manufacturers of automobile tires — Goodrich, Goodyear, and Firestone

These Big 3 were facing competition from Japan, which wanted to not only make their own tires, but also to buy the U.S. tire manufacturers. The U.S. tire makers were facing higher manufacturing costs due to the higher lending rates in the 1970s and higher wages incurred by labor and their unions. Does this sound similar to today's economy?

Employers and labor unions had fought hard for decades to secure stability for blue-collar workers in the form of wages, benefits, and pensions; however, these items were costing the companies a great deal and shareholders were responding accordingly. Shareholders applied downward pressure on stock values by selling off shares deemed to have lost value in the face of rising benefits that threatened company profits.

THE BUSINESS OF HEALTH INSURANCE

As mentioned in the previous chapter, Blue Cross and Blue Shield (BCBS) plans had expanded across more than 30 states and offered health insurance/benefits to individuals and employers. Once charging 50 cents/month, these plans were now charging much higher "premiums" to individuals and to employers. These premiums were established by BCBS accountants and actuaries, who ran multiple models to account for how much revenue from premiums would remain after payments were made for health services (i.e., the claims). This would result in net income (i.e., profit) for these insurance companies.

As an aside, be aware that while insurance companies generate net income from the pool of money after all expenses are paid (e.g., claims, salaries, rents, debt, etc.), they also operate in secondary markets and generate investment income similar to any large business through stocks, bonds, etc. For reference, the health insurance industry reported a 38% ($2 billion) increase in net investment income earned in 2022.[1]

What is unique to the insurance industry, however, is the ability to shift the risk of too many dollars paid out in claims to another insurer. This is known as reinsurance. In so doing, the insurers need slightly less capital or cash on hand to satisfy regulators, whose job is to ensure that insurers remain solvent to pay claims and can continue to keep premiums affordable to gain a bigger market of either individuals or employers.

For additional basic reading about the modern insurance industry, please see the insurance handbook referenced at the end of the book.[2]

It is also worth noting that these business practices exist (and under massive regulation) regardless of whether a company insures a loss to your home, auto, life, disability, or health. The main difference, however, is that when a claim is made on the former items, the beneficiary typically is paid directly for the financial loss. Notwithstanding payments made to the body shop when your car needs a repair, or to the roofer when a disaster causes a leak, many times the claimant is the direct recipient of the benefit (adjusted, of course, by claims adjusters).

In health insurance, however, the payment for the claim goes to the provider (e.g., hospital, physician, lab) who cared for your health. Of course, there are instances when you incur an expense for your healthcare, in which case you are reimbursed directly, and/or the more common instance where you bear a share of the cost in the form of a co-pay or co-insurance at least until a deductible is met, but the bulk of payment is made to the provider by the insurance company.

The point here is that health insurance is its own business, subject to all of the forces of any business, and is quite an intricate one to say the least. The service that the insurance companies sell is the insurance, but the deliverable is the "claim." That is what is produced by the company as its core business of providing a "goods and services." The total payment of claims is what the companies must deliver based on the good that was purchased. Healthcare insurance does not provide health; it provides a product to the marketplace that is paying for its service.

Suffice to say, by the 1970s, the system had evolved to the point that money flowed from one business (e.g., tire manufacturer) to another (e.g., BCBS) to another (e.g., hospital). The patient was more or less a bystander hoping that their "health" outcome was a good one.

Fundamentally, however, it was incumbent on all parties to ensure the "health" was managed appropriately by all purchasers and sellers of the services toward a favorable outcome for ALL vested parties, not just the patient. Health began to have a price tag. A value. One that was essentially bought and sold, just as Mr. Sloan so eloquently stated in 1929 and, as such, a "commodity" that would have profound impacts on the production of other goods and services. Later in the book we will explore how this notion of health as a commodity, as something that has value, will influence the new stakeholders in healthcare.

We learned in Chapter 2 that BCBS began as a prepayment for healthcare. Between the 1930s and 1950s, BCBS relied on providers (physicians and hospitals) to submit charge lists based entirely on cost. BCBS then defined what it would pay based on the defined procedure and what might be considered the average of charges submitted.

At the time, there was no widespread use of contracts or price negotiations as we know it today (more on that later). By 1955, nearly 70% of employed individuals had health benefit plans, in large part due to legislative changes in taxation rules that benefited both employers and employees.[3]

BCBS AND THE CHANGING RULES OF PAYMENT

In the late '70s, Miriam Fischer had worked her way up from a medical/laboratory technologist at the hospital in downtown Akron to the manager role. In 1983, she was offered a brand-new role in a brand-new entity known as the Health Maintenance Organization (HMO) of BCBS. This business had recently built a large corporate-looking medical facility that housed laboratory services, imaging services, and physicians' offices. As a manager, Miriam would oversee the lab and receive a 20% increase in salary compared to the hospital, as well as better benefits such as lower costs for her share of health insurance.

The HMO was an attempt by BCBS to begin to *manage the payments* it was making for outpatient and inpatient claims on services. It would be the equivalent of Dr. Ballard's patients deciding to pay him tomatoes, chickens, or other agricultural products, rather than cash or Louis Fischer deciding to give the physicians and administrators caring for his wife fine tailored suits. In other words, the payer of the claim (in this case the insurer) responsible for paying the bill decided to change the rules a bit in their favor.

In October 1983, BCBS of Ohio began the CURE (Controlling Utilization Results Effectively) program, which required approval before a patient was admitted to the hospital.[4] Naturally this requirement was highly criticized by physicians and hospitals, however the program saved BCBS of Ohio $40 million in its first year.[4]

In 1985, BCBS of Ohio required that hospitals bid for its "business" — that they bid for the guarantees of revenues that Kimball had worked so hard to establish for Baylor University Hospital 56 years earlier! And despite fierce opposition by clinicians, the State of Ohio provided legislative protection to health insurers by granting them the right to negotiate and contract payments to hospitals.

The facts of that era showed that BCBS' programs and strategies, in fact, lowered its expenses. What has been challenging to unravel, though, is who truly benefitted from these newfound savings. Clearly the insurer could show a better balance sheet to those who were invested in the company, including state offices of regulation and insurance who all had vested interests in keeping an eye on insurance companies. If those savings were passed along to employers/employees in the form of lowered premiums (which also was the desired architecture of state regulators, or at least limiting premium rate hikes), then those stakeholders benefitted as well.

It also forced hospitals and physicians to be more mindful of their own overhead expenses and to be more efficient in their operations. And, finally, at the same time, BCBS broke ground (literally and figuratively) on their own facility to provide ancillary services such as labs and imaging *at its own cost*, thereby directly competing with other providers. To top it off, they employed their own physicians to see the patients who were covered under BCBS plans.

When BCBS rolled out their plans to the major Ohio industries, including the auto and tire manufacturers, there was broad acceptance from labor and management and the HMO model took off.

Finally, Medicare began participating in these HMOs, and Medicare beneficiaries could avail themselves of an HMO plan so as to have better coverage for services than they could obtain with Medicare alone without any supplemental insurance.

THE BASICS OF MEDICARE

With the assumption that most physician leaders have a working knowledge of the history and basic structure of Medicare, I will not devote any significant time to that background (as that would be its own book all by itself), but suffice to say, we must address a few basic notions before we go much further in our understanding of the flow of money in healthcare and how, as a CMO, you must play a unique role in that current.

In 1965, just 20 years before the birth of the BCBS HMO in Ohio, under the leadership of President Lyndon B. Johnson, Congress enacted Medicare under Title XVIII of the Social Security Act to provide health insurance to people aged 65 and older, regardless of income or medical history.

For our purposes, keep in mind two things about that time in our history: (1) the number of U.S. citizens over the age of 65 was only 17 million (which would balloon to 55 million by 2021), and (2) the first coronary artery bypass graft (CABG) in the United States did not occur until 1964, under the leadership of Dr. Michael DeBakey at Baylor University Hospital.[5,6] By 1979, there were 114,000 CABG procedures per year in the U.S.[6]

Medicare was a blessing for the elderly who were not working and therefore not receiving employer-based health insurance, or for whom the cost of purchasing their own insurance was out of reach, which was often the case as actuaries deemed the premiums to be about three times the amount for a younger person.[7]

Again, beyond the scope of this chapter, be aware that Medicare was originally funded by taxes levied upon employers and employees (and is largely still funded that way today), but that the amount of claims paid by Medicare is exceeding the amount that has been collected (inclusive of investment growth of the fund that holds those tax dollars). So, it is somewhat analogous to commercial insurance in that workers are paying for a benefit (albeit deferred to a later age) to lessen the personal cost to their savings when they need care. Accordingly, therefore, Medicare also began to adjust its payments to reflect the increasing costs of providing care to those in need, but we will get to that in a moment.

In the early days of Medicare (1960s–late 1970s), the government program paid the hospitals and physicians based on the ongoing usual and customary fees set by those providers *and* allowed both to bill Medicare beneficiaries the amount in excess of Medicare's payment.[7] By 1975, annual increases in physician fees were allowed but based on changes in overall overhead of the provider work (materials, supplies, etc.).

Then, between 1984 and 1991, the yearly change in fees was determined by legislation because physician fees were rising faster than projected.[7] In 1992, the Medicare Fee Schedule was created with a list of about 7,000 services that could be billed and began to set limits on the ability to "balance bill" (asking the patient to pay the portion that Medicare would not cover).[7]

SETTING THE STAGE FOR TODAY'S ENVIRONMENT

In 1960, nearly 56% of all healthcare costs were paid by the patient; by 2012, that number had dropped to 12% due to the overwhelming growth of these third parties (government and non-government "commercial" insurers).[8] Along with the increased volume of covered consumers who could now avail themselves of medical care with less financial barriers than in the past, the elderly population was increasing and also now living longer because of advances in costly care (e.g., CABG).

These factors prompted a significant step up in the utilization of healthcare, not to mention the associated costs, both of which continue to today. They also marked the beginning of efforts *to* exert downward pressure onto payments made to hospitals and physicians. These two forces — increasing utilization (which is tied to cost) and decreasing payment — have battled diametrically for more than 30 years and have set the conditions for our modern experience.

LESSONS LEARNED

- Third-party payments are the engine and the brakes on a system that is moving rapidly. No U.S. model today eliminates the third party — the intermediary — as the means of splitting the money.
- Money flows to the intermediary from government sources (ultimately taxes) and/or businesses.
- The money held in the hands of the intermediary is what is drawing the attention of investors into healthcare. For the entire healthcare system to remain solvent, there must always be more money in the hands of the intermediary.
- Commercial insurance is a business structure that helps a variety of successful businesses thrive in local economies and in macroeconomies.
- Medicare is a social insurance program that protects individuals against risks experienced during aging — particularly illness-related financial insecurity. It is "insurance" because it pools risk. It is "social" because it pools money from society to protect members of society who would not otherwise be able to purchase the cost of care by themselves or the cost of insurance to cover that care.
- CMOs are a rare type of administrator/executive leader who, because of their clinical training, generally are the only ones who have first-hand knowledge of what the dollars actually are purchasing: knowledge, skills, competency, quality, and performance.

QUESTIONS TO ASK

- How many contracts does your organization have with third-party payers?
- Does your organization see those contracts as assets or liabilities?
- Who is involved in the negotiations with payers when contracts are being discussed?

- If you work in a medical group or a clinic, would you ever consider working in an integrated system that manages a volume of pooled money as well as the risk?
- Does your city depend on healthcare as an economic force? Are you part of the local economic development council?

CHAPTER 4

Billing, Claims, Collections

"With data collection, 'the sooner the
better' is always the best answer."

Marissa Mayer, CEO, Yahoo

IN 1975, THE SAME YEAR that Miriam Fischer left Pennsylvania for
Ohio, Dr. Arthur "Art" Staley had just finished his internal medicine
residency at the University of Cincinnati and opened up his practice
in an unassuming medical office in the Buchtel neighborhood, a few
miles west of downtown Akron.

Staley had grown up in Medina, Ohio, and had always dreamed
of becoming a physician and practicing medicine somewhere in
Northeast Ohio. He chose the Buchtel neighborhood so he could
serve multiple areas and have a multifaceted patient population.
He could serve the local residents, whether they worked in an
office building, a nearby factory, the local university, or simply the
surrounding suburban neighborhoods. As his reputation grew and
word spread of his calm demeanor, some of his patients drove 15–20
miles from nearby farm towns to see him.

As with many independent practices of the time, there were only
a few staff members in the office: a receptionist, a nurse and/or
medical assistant, and an office manager. To the office manager, this
mixture of patients would ultimately be known as the payer mix,
the lifeblood of any successful practice. It would also be the source
of tremendous complexity and the beginning of the next tectonic
shift in the business of medicine.

Recall that when Henry "Puff" Ballard and Bill Nadeau began
practicing medicine, they and their respective hospitals could charge
their patients fees, similar to any small or large business that provided a service, and expect payment in return.

As strange as it may sound, think about a beauty salon. The
charge for your haircut is based on the costs of the items used and

the service delivered, including the time in the chair, the electricity used, the amount of shampoo to lather your head, the amount of water used to wash and rinse, etc.

In such a setting, as the owner, you need nothing more than a cash register (or even just the till) and a way to record the invoice, payment, and receipt. In theory, you cover all of your expenses (electricity, water, rent, supplies) and the labor time/service (e.g., haircut in the chair) each day and have money left over to put in your pocket for transportation, groceries, and housing.

But imagine for a moment, that a client arrives for a full service (e.g., shampoo, rinse, cut, color, blow out) the next day and asks you to prepare a bill and send it to Omaha! The next client tells you to send an itemized bill to Detroit. And so on and so on.

At the end of every day, when you go to your office in the back of the salon, you must track every bill that was sent and whether or not you received payment. To top it off, every time you receive payment from Omaha or Detroit, it comes in a bundle reflecting multiple clients for a period of time and it is up to you to ensure that every bill was paid for each and every customer and for each and every item that you charged!

THE COMPLEXITIES OF MOVING THE MONEY

Dr. Staley needed not just a bevy of patients in 1975, he needed a competent manager to sort through all of the various payers for his services. Each factory worker, university teacher, or farmer likely had a different insurer covering the cost of their medical care, and each insurance company had different requirements regarding how to submit the bill and when to expect payment — all of which varied from the newly formed Medicare.

Needless to say, Dr. Staley and his office team did well and thrived for at least 10 years under those circumstances. This was also true for Akron's General Hospital, which functioned in much the same manner. But as companies recovered from the stagnant economy of the 1970s, along came the impact and the power of computing.

Until that time, much of the accounting for businesses large and small was manual and on paper. With the introduction of computers, certain tasks could be automated, accomplished faster, done more efficiently, and with increasing complexity, resulting in better data management.

As things began to heat up with more insurers to interact with and with rapidly changing rules and requirements generated by the insurers, office managers were forced to hire more staff and/or purchase computers to keep up.

These increasing expenses for the physician office were passed along to all payers in the form of increased usual and customary fees. In response to physician fees rising more quickly than expected in order to keep up with the new medical payment micro-environment, legislation was enacted in 1984 to manage those fees.[1]

The shift in medical payments that began in the mid-1980s was much like the chicken and the egg paradox. Which came first? Were rising expenses increasing the payments or were payments increasing the expenses? Just as the physicians and hospitals were trying to manage their own expenses and maintain a steady profit, the insurers were managing more payments due to more patients being cared for and to advances in medicine resulting in an increasing use of services. I will not opine on how this cycle first started, or if any side bears the ultimate responsibility for the origin point but suffice to say payers and service providers were inextricably linked and remain so 40 years later.

Why were physician offices suddenly scrambling to keep up with the constant changes (e.g., computerized billing processes) mandated by the payers? As increasing utilization lead to increasing payments, upper management tasked insurance employees to reduce over-payment that was linked to errors, waste, and fraud. Any over-payment disrupted the earnings of the insurance company and subsequently to shareholders. Likewise, any inefficiency on the part of the insurance company that caused net income to drop could prompt those companies to charge more for their service in the form of higher premiums to companies that were purchasing/sponsoring those plans for its employees.

Higher premiums generated new risks for all parties; they could decrease market share for the insurance company (and company viability) if factories and school systems would no longer enter into agreements with the insurance company or if the employers would pass those new costs on to either their employees for their share of the insurance coverage or into the price of its product (e.g., tires, automobiles), which could weaken its market share and so on and so on. Just as the independent physician practice had to mind its shop on a daily basis, so, too, did the insurance company, just on a much bigger scale.

Approximately 14% of a primary care physician's professional revenue is devoted to the work involved with billing and collections.[2] So, for every dollar received, 14 cents are dedicated to paying the expense of sending out a bill to a third party. It has been suggested that there are six discrete steps when generating a claim following the physician encounter in order to arrive at a receipt of payment.[2] Likewise, insurance companies spend a tremendous amount of time adjudicating and adjusting those claims for payment, so a percentage of its revenue from premium dollars is devoted to the management of the physician claim.

In effect, both sides of the payment structure put a tremendous amount of time, energy, and expense into how the money moves from the payer to the service provider. Multiply that process across all of the various payers and it is clear why the overall cost of healthcare in the United States is higher than in other countries that have less duplicative payer models.[3]

It is important to understand, however, that the movement of the money from one party to another carries a cost to both sides. Later, we will explore how this creates opportunities for both parties.

INSURERS AS MONEY MANAGERS

Dr. Staley was a tall, calm man who was widely respected for his diagnostic skills. He treated his patients with an almost effortless amount of empathy and understanding and remained focused on the art of medicine. His business skills were good, but as the early 1980s unfolded, he realized the complexities of the practice were catching up with his entrepreneurial limits.

He met with his office manager weekly to review and discuss the practice, but the meetings were taking longer and longer and he began to feel some pressure to change something to keep the *status quo*.

BCBS had just begun to leverage its political and economic position and to make stipulations about what services would be covered under its member benefit agreements.[4] One stipulation came in the form of pre-registration or prior authorization and was a highly effective "stop sign" at the intersection of patient traffic and hospital/physician services.

Early on, much of the new requirements would simply slow down the service occurrence, but in some cases, merely by the nature of attrition ("giving up") the services would never be rendered for fear of lack of payment to the provider or fear that the patient could not/would not be able to afford an uncovered service.

This behavior by the insurance company is a source of great consternation for physicians and patients. In the past, under the general principles of professionalism and licensure, it was the social norm to believe that both sides behaved appropriately in the transaction of medical service. When Dr. Henry "Puff" Ballard's receptionist asked the patient for payment, there was no methodology for the patient to examine the legitimacy of the invoice. Was the diagnosis accurate, was the treatment effective, was the outcome of benefit?

But as with so many things in the modern age, as the system became more complex, the intermediate layers evolved to provide internal checks and balances to manage the actual transaction. As Dr. Staley's practice was maturing, insurers were beginning to use a strategy under the auspices of oversight and fiduciary responsibility.

The moral hazard for insurers — and all third-party payers, for that matter — is to reconcile their responsibilities to those that pay the premium and to those that are invested, directly or indirectly, in the business.

Insurers are perceived nowadays as arbiters of health; however, that perception is open to ongoing debate. Rather, in my opinion, insurers are the arbiters of the exchange of money between multiple stakeholders.

It is imperative, therefore, that the CMO, no matter whether they work for a payer or a provider, be as realistic and as pragmatic as possible when facing the tensions that exist around the splitting of the money among stakeholders. To be caught up in politics, positions, or rhetoric around this does a disservice to a whole host of people who genuinely work hard at their jobs facilitating the flow of healthcare payments.

Introducing Managed Care

Previously, prices were set by the physician or the hospital. In the 1980s, however, the commercial insurance companies began to roll out "managed care" in the form of prior authorizations and with the imposition of new limits on payments. As described above, insurers were attempting to address increasing payments to maintain a degree of *status quo* from their economic perspective. Gone were the days of paying the "usual and customary."

BCBS and other payers, including Medicare with the physician fee schedule beginning in 1992, were able to effectively enforce price controls on services by entering into agreements with physicians about the pricing of services. These pricing agreements were a new method of stabilizing the efflux from the payers.

Managing the Office Processes

Getting back to Dr. Staley's practice, the office manager and her team had developed a reasonable method of tracking all claims for which it expected to get paid, otherwise known as accounts receivable (A/R), but it became harder and harder to actually "scrub" the claims for errors that would cause the payers to deny the claims and to be sure that each claim was paid accurately and at the right time.

Not surprisingly, Dr. Staley's office manager advised him to enter into agreements with insurers to continue to see the influx of cash into his office. Because he had to give up control over the prices his office could charge, it was therefore decided that by seeing an additional patient or two each day, he could make up for decrease in payment.

Also, under these new agreements, there may be different fee allowances for each patient encounter, claims systems, and dates of payments. Thus, the A/R tracking became increasingly complicated, such that it took even more effort to scrub the charge on the claim, the "allowed" charge that would actually be paid, the amount that was actually paid, and when it was paid.

The last part was probably the most frustrating because payers had a tremendous amount of latitude to "hold" payments to ensure that they had scrubbed everything on their end before releasing payment — not to mention that the payers often sent lump payments for all of the claims that were finally scrubbed and considered "clean," such that now the office or hospital had to match every outgoing claim to every received payment to be sure that it was accurately disbursed.

In many cases, there were patients, insured or self-paid, who were not able to pay their share because of loss of job, income, re-location, etc., so attaining a collection rate of 100% was practically impossible.

For accurate forecasting, budgeting, and paying employees of the hospital or practice in a timely manner, revenue managers also needed to oversee "days in A/R" — the average time that it takes to be paid by the responsible party — which, combined with collections, could approximate the amount of cash available to meet payroll or other expenses.

Whether an organization manages payroll inhouse or outsources to a third party, the organization must fund payroll from cash or another source, like a line of credit, which charges an interest rate on the borrowed money. Carrying cost, borrowing cost, and outsourcing place greater expense back to the practice. The decision to use cash, borrow cash, or invest the cash has a fundamental impact on the financial performance of any business, especially a small medical practice.

CODES, CLASSIFICATIONS, AND ACCOUNTABILITY

Just as pricing began to slide away from physician control and the workload, and the cost to maintain the *status quo* increased, the effort required to bring in the money became increasingly laborious (and also increased practice overhead).

Let's return to the hair salon for just a moment. Imagine that after your client requested that you send your bill to Omaha, the folks in Omaha returned the bill and said that the form used to request payment was incomplete. The form required the exact length of hair removed, the color of hair, the thickness of the hair, the type of hair (curly, wavy, or straight), and the location of the hair removed (bangs, sides, neckline, etc.). What's more, all of those variables and descriptors must be formatted into numbers or codes.

This is essentially what happened in the world of medical payment and it started in 1948, when the International Classification of Diseases (ICD) was taken over by the World Health Organization.[5] At its inception in the 1800s, the ICD was a means by which scientists could classify and track diseases to better understand them. After several centuries and multiple iterations, in 1977, ICD-9 (version 9) became the standard classification of disease and was used for almost 38 years, until ICD-10 was rolled out in 2015.[5] The latest version, ICD-11, was adopted and went into effect in January 2022.

Similarly, in 1966, a complex interplay between the newly created Centers for Medicare and Medicaid Services (CMS) and the American Medical Association (AMA), resulted in the creation of Current Procedural Terminology (CPT).[5]

While originating as a classification for procedures and services to help track and manage data, the CPT is now the set of codes that are used to describe what actually occurred during a patient encounter and that is required for the submission of claims.

The combined ICD-11 codes to identify the diseases or conditions and the CPT codes to establish procedures performed are processed and converted into a billing algorithm that is used to create a claim for the service(s) rendered.

Today, ICD and CPT codes are the two elements that are required for all inpatient and outpatient services and are the basis for ensuring that physicians are paid for their professional services. Although there are many more nuances around physician coding, suffice to say that physician payments transitioned from analog documentation and simplified billing to digitized elements and complex billing during the second half of the 20th century.

PAYING HOSPITALS

Hospitals were not spared this shift either. On October 1, 1983, payments to hospitals in the United States were upended by CMS, when the prospective payment system (PPS) was implemented in response to rising costs of hospital care.[6] A PPS is a reimbursement strategy in which Medicare payment is made based on a predetermined, fixed amount.

Following work done by the Yale University Hospital system and the success of a PPS in New Jersey, Congress legislated that CMS would adopt a payment model for hospitals that would be based on specific conditions and payments would be made in accordance with another classification system of diseases known as diagnostic related groups (DRGs).[6] The DRG sorts patients that are clinically coherent by disease group and homogeneous with respect to resource use.

The PPS is designed to pay the hospital for the discharge of the patient's condition, as determined by the classification of each case into a DRG. Such a classification scheme allows for equitable payment across hospitals in that comparable services can be comparably remunerated.

Imagine, once more, that in the hair salon, Omaha will now pay only one rate for all pixie cuts, regardless of how much hair is removed, coloring applied, or straightening required. In other words, the stylist has to be mindful of how much time is spent in the chair, how much dye is used, and how much to apply the curling iron/flattener because only one price will be paid for a pixie cut regardless of the effort that went into it.

In the hospital, the payment rates for each DRG are determined in advance and they constitute payment in full for the care received in the hospital. As such, the hospital loses money or profits from these payments, depending on how it manages the cost of the care. And just like in the commercial insurance industry in the 1980s, CMS was attempting to apply pressure on the rising costs and expenditures of the Medicare program due to the ever-increasing aging population, new services, chronic diseases, and increasing net utilization.

As in the outpatient world, increasing digitization (i.e., coding) was applied to the processes of payments which, in turn, increased the administrative overhead of the hospital revenue cycle management departments.

By the 1980s, the processes physicians and hospitals were required to undertake in order to be paid increased, creating tension between those who delivered the services and those who held the payments. This tension has continued for the past 40 years and has spawned a number of interlopers and middlemen who continue to change how the money in healthcare is ultimately split.

LESSONS LEARNED

- Kimball's original design of a third-party payer was initiated to ensure money was placed into a pool such that risk was shared by all participants. By sharing risk, all stakeholders would have their needs met and neither the patient nor the hospital would be severely impacted by the cost of the care.
- As utilization increased, so did the complexity of the risk. Consequently, those who were responsible for managing risk produced managed care processes.
- Price controls began through legislation or pricing agreements (i.e., contracts) as a tactic to manage the available pool of money from which to share risk.
- In parallel with pricing arrangements, the processes have evolved from simplistic analog to digital involving classification codes and procedural codes.
- The increasing complexities of pricing, billing, and claims payment has shifted more risk (in terms of dollar management) of every patient encounter to the provider side. To receive the same revenue as in the past, the provider (whether physician, clinic, or hospital) must increase its volume of service, its overhead directed toward charge management, and

the surveillance of cash flow in proportion to its own activity. All of those activities increase provider overhead that must also be managed or else the provider ends up in an upward cycle of workload without end.

QUESTIONS TO ASK

- As a CMO, do you find yourself taking sides when it comes to discussions revolving around payers vs. providers?
- If so, are you able to re-frame the discussion so it is "yes, and" rather than "either or"? Can you establish the connection points?
- How do you respect the environment of how the money travels when you neither designed it nor are currently empowered to unwind it?
- How do you engage with your physician colleagues when this interplay of the payer and the provider causes stress and friction? What about the friction in the C-suite or boardroom?
- Can you hold opposing forces in your mind and in your discussions loosely so as to arrive at conclusions that support the mission of your organization?
- Are you stuck in a predatory and invective environment regarding payment structures?
- What percent of revenue at your organization is devoted to billing, coding, claims, utilization, collections, etc.? How much of every dollar is "spent" on capturing a dollar? How much money is at stake in each area? In what areas should the CMO have responsibility? Influence?
- Are you empowered to intervene and reduce the ever-increasing workload on physicians related to payment structures? If not, why not? Can you or should you intercede and seek some authority or influence on the matter?

CHAPTER 5

Supply, Supplies, and Demands

"We make a living by what we get,
but we make a life by what we give."
Winston Churchill

OVER HIS 10 YEARS IN BUCHTEL, Dr. Staley began to note a subtle change in his practice. Some of his longtime patients were choosing to go elsewhere for their care and the rate of new patients entering the practice was trending down ever so slightly. Both of these subtleties were occurring while his overall expenses were creeping up and he was trying to see more patients month over month to keep the practice income stable.

One of his patients was Miriam Fischer, who once worked at Akron's General Hospital, and now worked at a new HMO medical facility in Fairlawn, a growing suburb west of Buchtel. One day while rounding early in the morning on his inpatients at General Hospital, he ran into Miriam's former boss, John, the head of laboratory services. Dr. Staley inquired if John knew how Miriam was doing working over in Fairlawn. The reply provided some insight into the very same subtleties occurring in the medical practice.

The new HMO was closer to Miriam's house and therefore a shorter daily commute. Her health insurance was an added benefit. As an employee of the newly created HMO, she had no co-pays and a very low deductible so long as all of her care was performed within the HMO network. Medications were quite affordable if she used the HMO's pharmacy program. Her workday was less hectic than in the hospital when seasonal volumes made the laboratory services rather busy, if not erratic.

Later, Dr. Staley discovered that several hospital employees had found jobs at the HMO facility and that some local industries had been switching their employer-sponsored health plan benefits to the new HMO plan. This was done for cost savings to the companies' bottom line and to their employees who were benefitting from one-stop shopping, lower co-pays, and lower deductibles.

Patients were ostensibly voting with their wallets and with their feet by choosing a new alternative to traditional care. Once inside the HMO medical office building, the patient experienced a new level of convenience with doctor visits, imaging, and lab services available all at once and with far lower out-of-pocket expense.

PHYSICIAN ROLES AND HMOs

When it comes to the role of physicians, HMOs have four models.[1]

1. *Staff models* are those in which the HMO hires its own physicians and sometimes owns a hospital, but this scenario is rare.

2. In *group models,* which are somewhat more common, the HMO contracts with a single physician group that provides all the clinical services rendered to the HMO subscribers (i.e., patients) and typically provides care *only* to the HMO subscribers. Kaiser-Permanente is a classic example of a group model.

3. Third, and most common, model is the *network model* in which the HMO-insurer contracts with several physician groups in the local market. Each physician group sees a significant number of the HMO's subscribers, but the groups also see patients from other insurers.

4. The *independent practice association (IPA) model* emerged local medical societies' response to the growth of HMOs. Under this model, the HMO-insurer provides services through a large panel of physicians throughout the community. For the most part, these models reflect the various market conditions of physician supply and demand in local communities and the ability to structure a model to best serve the members enrolled in the insurance plan.

Given the recent office practice demands around payer contracts, differential payments, and the ever-increasing overhead just to keep the most of every dollar and maintain a stable income, Dr. Staley decided it was time to take stock of the landscape and re-consider his next move.

He contemplated whether to expand his practice in any number of ways. He could hire a young physician who would bring in more dollars, paying the new doctor at a lower salary than his own, at least for a while. He could add a nurse practitioner much in the same way. He could even add office-based services that were reimbursable and would bring in extra cash. Or he could simply consider working at the newly formed staff model HMO in Fairlawn.

When he considered the pros and cons of building his own business versus learning more about the business of healthcare and which environment would enable him to focus on his love of patient care and the art of medicine, he chose employment at the HMO in Fairlawn.

After signing an employment agreement and selling his practice to a small group of internists located close to the hospital, Dr. Staley went to work at the HMO. For a couple of years he was pleased with his choice.

Further, given his decade of experience in private practice and his newfound interest in the business of healthcare, Dr. Staley was appointed as medical director of the HMO for the Akron market. His responsibilities included managing physician contracts, utilization, clinical practices, claims reviews, denials management support, and peer-to-peer authorizations, all on behalf of the parent insurer of the HMO.

As far as his practice went, he was seeing roughly the same number of patients as in private practice but without the worry of keeping the practice afloat. His prior practice weekly meetings with his office manager were replaced by all of the administrative duties mentioned above. And Miriam, along with many other former patients who were HMO members, returned to his care under the HMO umbrella.

HMOs and HEALTHCARE CONSTRAINTS

Not long after Dr. Staley settled into the routines of this new environment, Miriam arrived at the clinic for an office visit. She had been more tired than usual lately, despite the fact that her role in the laboratory had not changed to any degree. Miriam described some pain and mild swelling in her left armpit.

On examination, Dr. Staley discovered left axillary adenopathy and wrote in his note that there were several easily palpable firm, fixed, and possibly matted nodes. A breast exam revealed a fullness with mass-like effect in the upper outer quadrant.

With a referral to a surgeon and a few basic tests, Miriam was diagnosed with locally advanced breast carcinoma and underwent a radical mastectomy, followed by a visit to the oncologist, all of which occurred at Akron's City Hospital. Miriam subsequently underwent months of intensive treatment at City Hospital, including radiation therapy.

For years, Dr. Staley had built his reputation at Akron's General Hospital, along with his referral patterns to physicians that he could trust, and Miriam had enjoyed the camaraderie of many co-workers while she was employed there. Neither Dr. Staley nor Miriam was entirely pleased with City Hospital, but that was the in-network provider for the HMO. So, the doctor and the patient, for different reasons, were extremely unsettled that care would be provided at the "rival" hospital, which, at least in the past, had slight reputation of providing inferior care.

COVERING EXPENSES AND SHIFTING RISK

In the 1980s and 1990s, as managed care blossomed, the notion of the insurer directing the patient to a particular site of clinical care was novel. This practice was widely criticized and labeled as interfering with the sacrosanct doctor-patient relationship, if not the actual practice of medicine. How did this happen?

Once more, we turn to the splitting up of the money. Recall that in this period, hospitals were now being paid by Medicare in a prospective manner based on the condition requiring hospitalization, as defined by the DRG coding. The legislative design of the prospective payment put downward pressure on hospitals to better manage the cost of care provided.

In much the same way, commercial insurers followed suit with efforts to create a prospective payment approach to hospital inpatient care for much the same reason: to stabilize expenses on their side and shift the risk of what ultimately happens to the dollars over to the hospital.

Unlike federal regulations that required hospitals to accept the Medicare payments, generally speaking there were no parallel rules that required hospitals to accept a mandated payment plan from private payers.[2] So, hospitals naturally pushed back on the private payers' proposed payment plans.

Recall that until this time, hospitals could invoice the insurer based on a very itemized bill for all types of services rendered to the patient, including food, medication, bed linens, procedures, etc. This was lucrative for the hospital, but insurers began to offer to pay flat rates for the entire stay based on conditions, much like Medicare.

Hospitals countered the flat rate concept with offers to pay the rate but at a certain percentage of the Medicare rate (e.g., 110%, 115%, etc.). Insurers counter-offered by dropping the now-inflated flat rate and returning to the itemized charges but at a discounted rate (e.g., 90% or 92.5%) of the initial charges for each item. In some cases, hospitals and insurers tried to split the difference and determine a "per-diem" rate — a daily payment for each day of the hospital stay.

Believe it or not, all three structures currently exist (prospective payments based on percent of Medicare, discounts of charges, and per-diem rates) between hospitals and private payers, although those negotiated rates and structures between the parties are generally tightly controlled "trade secrets."[3]

A Challenge for Insurers

Data show that these downward pressures on hospitals changed how hospital care was delivered, namely with decreased length of stays, lower rates of admissions, and lower overall utilization of services.[2] Hospitals now had to manage care to meet the payment structure and to find the most cost-effective means to do so. This is precisely what the government and private sector wanted in order to lower their expenditures.

At the same time, though, the unintended consequences of the federal mandates pushed the risk management over to the private sector. Since there were no pricing mandates backing up the private sector, hospitals could seek higher and higher payments from the private insurance market through contract negotiations. Private practitioners running small offices had no leverage in this arena; however, the hospitals had tremendous advantages.

Commercial insurers looking to maintain a diversified pool of members (which lowers risk) do so by having as many opportunities as possible to serve as the employer's or employees' insurer of choice. Insurers want to sell health plans that provide comprehensive services and affordable co-payments to as many clients as possible. Employers seek cost-effective benefits to maintain an engaged workforce. The net result is that insurers must meet the demands of the employers who purchase their products, but this places them at a disadvantage to the hospitals who provide the service.

As one example of this strength, hospitals can opt out of any contract. This opt-out maneuver then forces the health plan company to seek services elsewhere, possibly a place that offers fewer services, is farther away, and possibly not as good of quality. On the insurer's side, in addition to negotiating a price or a payment model that the two sides agree upon, the insurer can offer to pay claims promptly and steer patients toward the hospital to continue its market share advantage.

Rising Operational Costs

Just as the office manager in the physician practice must manage different fees, different payment arrangements, and different timeliness of payments, so do the hospitals, and all of this increases the administrative overhead of the hospital operation.

One of the most challenging aspects of the U.S. healthcare system as it has evolved in the last century, is that as downward pressures continue regarding payments from CMS, the operational costs naturally rise, and one of the only ways to support the operating margin is for hospitals to charge private payers more than they are permitted to charge the government.[4]

In the 1980s and 1990s, physicians could make up revenue by seeing more patients or offering more services. Similarly, hospitals began to take advantage of the prospective payments by shifting care to less-expensive locations, but still under the auspices of the hospital, such as hospital outpatient care departments (HOPD).[4,5]

Under HOPD rules, the hospital could ostensibly receive rates equivalent to inpatient care, even if the services were done as an outpatient where the care was considerably less expensive due to lower overhead costs such as electricity, water, and workforce.

It became clear to hospitals that the expansion of services beyond the traditional inpatient wards and operating rooms could boost the net income, as payments would continue and/or improve, but the services were accomplished with less direct overhead.

To add insult to injury, physicians who were trying at the same time to create new services could not bill at an HOPD rate, but rather at what is known as "provider-based billing." Although physician practice expenses are lower than those of hospitals, the payment rates are also lower. Now hospitals and physicians were competing for the same added services, but under different economic conditions.

When Miriam began her chemotherapy at City Hospital, she was admitted for several days each month for infusion therapy, intense monitoring, and aggressive hydration because of the profound effects of the anthracycline-based regimen. City Hospital and the HMO had negotiated a fixed per-diem rate for Miriam's care, but City Hospital lost money each day due to the cost of the medications, hydration, and efforts to manage her side effects.

Hospitals had long been in the habit of purchasing their pharmaceutical supplies in bulk as a way to achieve some type of discount; however, oftentimes the standard discount would be neutralized if the patient required medications around the clock, such that the volume of use would negate the value of the discount.

Recall that under a flat per-diem rate (regardless the rate), once all of the costs exceeded the daily rate, the hospital was no longer generating any profitable margin. When Miriam required radiation therapy, she was able to receive this in the outpatient department and was not as ill as when she was receiving chemotherapy. This meant that she could have daily treatments without hospitalization, but the hospital would still receive a payment under HOPD billing that more than made up for the shortfall when Miriam was an inpatient.

For several years, Miriam's disease appeared to be in remission; however, in 1991, she was found to have multiple bone metastasis along with evidence of liver involvement. Once more, she was hospitalized for intensive multi-drug chemotherapy, benefitting from the newly approved 5HT3 antagonist ondansetron, which greatly improved her anti-emesis interventions.

While good news for Miriam, and presumably resulting in shorter hospital stays, this new pharmaceutical product cost the hospital an extraordinary amount of money to purchase. And even though City Hospital was under the new per-diem contract with the HMO, once more the hospital found itself losing money, since it had no direct way of passing the cost of the medication on to the payer (unlike the 1930s and 1940s).

While the new contract was modified to take into account the rapid changes in healthcare, it did not have any type of itemized billing to pass along new costs to the payer. This scenario played itself out not just in oncology, but also in many areas of specialty care as new and expensive drugs emerged.

Additionally, newer more expensive infusion devices, infusion pumps, catheters, prostheses, and more all came along at a time when hospitals were no longer able to use itemized charges to cover the costs of these products and services.

Group Purchase Organizations

By no means were hospitals going bankrupt, but the pressures of utilizing these new products and services came with inherent costs, particularly in relation to supplies. Naturally, hospitals began to create more services that could be delivered in the outpatient setting in order to bill with lower expenses under HOPD, and they found ways to increase their purchasing power through group purchase organizations (GPOs). These GPOs acted like any other bulk buyer of goods (think of Sam's Club or Costco), such that by buying in bulk from manufacturers and by offering them prompt payment, the GPOs pass those savings to the hospitals in the form of discounts and/or rebates on a wide range of pharmaceuticals and medical supplies.[6]

In fact, some of the rebate structure was enabled through legislation for the very reason that costs were increasing: in order to better serve the Medicare beneficiaries who were being pinched by higher prices when in need of medications prescribed outside of the inpatient care.[6] Better than charging item by item, hospitals could purchase these items at lower costs and "pocket" the difference.

Lastly, hospitals had one more purchasing advantage in the form of the 340b program, another federally legislated program that forced manufacturers to provide discounted products to hospitals serving a particular share of the most vulnerable patients.[7] Further, the program protected these hospitals by allowing them to charge standard prices and to keep the difference between the reimbursed amount and the discounted purchase price.[7]

Payments and pricing, and the responses to both, became a vortex of payers and providers scrambling to keep as much of the dollar that they received for their delivered product. In today's vernacular, this is often referred to as "misaligned incentives."

LESSONS LEARNED

- Hospitals initially held an advantage over private payers because they controlled the bulk of services that patients required. The advantages created the negotiated pricing models.
- Since government payment was relatively fixed, if hospitals saw narrow margins in the care of Medicare beneficiaries, even after attempting greater operational efficiencies, they could press private payers for higher payments to make up the difference and increase overall margins.
- Private commercial insurers responded accordingly to the hospital pricing with ever more complex structures for local care (e.g., the early HMO models) to better "manage" the money flow.

- The more complex and varying payment structures required more complex administrative systems to move the money from one place to another. This became a significant cost added to the cost of care.
- Physicians faced similar challenges, and some created larger enterprises to capture more revenue, at least to cover the growing administrative overhead.
- Hospitals entered into several decades of exploring and exploiting various ways to trim costs, obtain material discounts, and capture more margin under fixed reimbursement.

QUESTIONS TO ASK

- How are medical products selected at your organization?
- How is your formulary established? By committee? How much physician representation exists in the selection of medications? Are the physicians elected, appointed, or otherwise selected to participate? What authority does the CMO have in this selection process?
- Who determines pathways and protocols for medication delivery in your organization?
- Are any savings passed on to patients? To the organization?
- What role should the CMO play in the purchase of medical products and supplies? What empowerment, if any, exists on behalf of physicians when products are evaluated?
- Should the CMO work with the supply chain leadership in your organization?
- Are there ways in which the CMO can intercede in the supply chain processes and realize savings for the organization?
- Are outpatient services better or worse for patient safety? Which ones are a win-win for the patient's health and the financial health of the organization?
- Should a CMO weigh in on new service lines or migration to outpatient services? Have all the laws of unintended consequences been evaluated as these decisions impact patient safety and quality?

- Should a CMO have authority over the site of service? Is there a clinical imperative involved (i.e., best practice?) or is it simply operationally more efficient? Or both?

CHAPTER 6

PPMs and MSOs

"It's far better to buy a wonderful company at a fair
price than a fair company at a wonderful price."

Warren Buffet

"What has been will be again, what has been done will
be done again; there is nothing new under the sun."

Ecclesiastes 1:9

IN 1992, DR. STALEY WAS INVITED to have lunch with the two
most-senior physicians among the group that now ran his old practice. The Akron Internal Medical Associates (AIMA) had grown and
now included not only internists, but also family practitioners, subspecialists, allergists, and a variety of others. The group was gaining
traction on their negotiating leverage with commercial payers now
that they cared for large numbers of patients and with a wide range
of services. They had created a laboratory and imaging, including
both CT and MRI as part of their growth.

The group was considering the addition of cardiologists, ortho-
pedists, and oncology to gain cardiac imaging, outpatient rehab,
and infusion therapy. It was the vision of the senior physicians to
expand the group to achieve greater stature when negotiating with
payers and also to grow additional sources of revenue for the group.

The physicians had invited Dr. Staley not just to share their
vision, but to ask him to return to the group as its COO. The older
of the two senior doctors would serve as CEO and the slightly
younger one as CFO. With Dr Staley's role at the HMO, they felt
certain that he could add great value and insight into the operations, particularly around payer contract negotiations and growth
of services.

Dr. Staley had become a bit disillusioned with the HMO of late.
At first, he enjoyed the freedom of not running a practice while still

learning about the "business of medicine," but slowly the HMO's impact on patient care was distressing him. He was bothered that he was not fully directing the flow of Miriam's care. While not critical of the care she was receiving, he missed the network of relationships he had built at General Hospital and the confidence that his patients would receive care from people he knew and trusted.

He was also pained that if Miriam sought to limit her out-of-pocket expenses, she had no input on her care and had to travel a little bit farther than was necessary to seek care at City Hospital rather than at General Hospital.

It took Dr. Staley only two days to make his decision. He announced his resignation at the Fairlawn HMO and provided two weeks' notice of his departure.

Once he settled in at AIMA's main office located near General Hospital, he found himself quite skilled at establishing the various projects that would recruit and integrate the three additional specialties and their respective ancillary revenue streams. In fact, after just two and a half years, the group had accomplished its goals. It had established itself as a major provider of services and was having an immediate impact on the two local hospitals regarding referrals for services and ease of use by patients. Correspondingly, the commercial insurers were taking notice as well.

ENTER: PHYSICIAN PRACTICE MANAGEMENT

Things seemed to be going well enough that the group leadership team began to formulate another strategic growth plan that would involve the addition of surgeons, surgical subspecialists (e.g., urology), and a joint venture for an ambulatory surgery center, and on really ambitious days, a radiation oncology services. While planning these initiatives, the CFO declared that with the recently added services and the proposed new services, the administrative costs were beginning to eat into AIMA's profitability.

Toward the end of the 1980s, a new trend emerged among medical groups in the form of physician practice management (PPM) companies that were created to help physicians handle complex new issues.

PPMs provided administrative services to medical groups and reduced physicians' financial risk in working with managed care contracts, particularly through greater clout in negotiating managed care contracts — exactly what the Akron medical group was trying to accomplish on its own. And when the CFO at AIMA announced the financial challenges facing the group, the executive team began to consider the role of a PPM.

When a PPM acquired a practice, it purchased assets in the form of equipment, accounts receivable, and, sometimes, real estate. Under a multi-year (20–40 years) contract, the PPM would manage the clinic for approximately 15% of revenues from physician fees after expenses and before physician salaries.[1]

Recall from Chapter 4 that administrative costs were eating up 14 cents of every dollar in an average primary care practice. For the doctors to reap the benefit, the arrangement with a PPM would have to show either lower overhead in the form of lower administrative costs (lower the numerator below the average of 14%) or improved up-front revenues (increasing the denominator of cash collections) in return for the 15% split of profit to the PPM.

When doctors sold their business to the PPM, the physicians received cash, stock, or both for their practices but remained independent and did not become employees of PPMs. In this way, they received an appropriate valuation for their practice success but still remained at "arm's length."

One such PPM, PhyCor, was founded in 1988 by four former executives from the Hospital Corporation of America (HCA) who knew a thing or two about the business of healthcare delivery.[1] PhyCor acquired the Nalle Clinic in Charlotte, North Carolina, in 1990 and revenues rose 30% the first year and 5–10% each year afterward for the first five years. The clinic grew to 106 doctors through the ongoing acquisitions of physician practices.[1,2]

Outsourcing Revenue Management

In addition to lower operating expenses through business acumen and applied management techniques, and along with increased revenues from better payer contracts and volumes of services, one of the attractions of selling a practice to a PPM involved the infusion of capital for equipment and facilities.

PhyCor, as a whole, represented a stronger borrower than small physician clinics and could continue to leverage its assets (medical buildings, accounts receivables, etc.) and supply clinic operators with more capital and/or cash to purchase more equipment or facilities.

Early on, medical groups who were seeking more bargaining power along with income preservation were attracted to PPMs. With national exposure, access to capital, cash back into physicians' pockets (through acquisition and/or better reimbursement), and only 15% of the physician fees in return, PPMs looked all too good.

After several months of discussions with potential PPM partners, Dr. Staley had his reservations, but ultimately agreed along with the CEO and CFO to present the Akron Internal Medical Associates' partners with an offer by a PPM to acquire the practice, along with some of its real estate and equipment lease obligations, in return for better contract negotiating, steady operational cash, and capital to fund further growth.

The pitch to the group was that of a major capital partner and a path forward for stability in incomes and the potential for increasing net revenues that, if profitable after expenses, could be distributed among the physician partners.

The idea of splitting money with a capital partner rather than seeing it go toward increasing administrative overhead went over very well among the partners in the medical group. No one asked the senior physicians if this was just a swap of expense management from the local control of the practice to a more remote control of the operations. No one asked if the PPM could do a better job given the early results at the other clinics thus far. It was believed that if success could happen in North Carolina, it could happen in Ohio.

So, for perhaps the first time in the late 20th century, we see the transition of physician revenue management to an outside vendor — an outsourcing of how to handle the flow of money — and investors acted accordingly.

Reaping the Benefits

After three years of operations, PhyCor revenues increased from $1.2 million in 1988 to $90 million by the end of 1991.[1] An initial public offering (IPO) of 2.5 million shares of stock at $16 per share raised $40 million for the purchase of additional multispecialty medical clinics.[1] With the acquisition of six medical practices, located throughout the United States, 1992 revenues reached $136 million through 14 clinics in nine states.[1]

PhyCor continued to acquire practices in the 1990s and naturally continued to see increases in revenues; then it saw an opportunity and leveraged its cash flow and assets to create additional companies.

One of the companies it added to its portfolio was PhyCor Management Corporation, formed to develop and manage independent practice associations (IPAs) — the loose organizational networks in which independent physicians contracted with managed care plans and shared management resources.[1]

GROWTH THROUGH MANAGED SERVICES ORGANIZATIONS

In February 1995, PhyCor purchased an existing company, North American Medical Management Company, Inc. (NAMM), which at the time provided only a small bundle of services (e.g., billing and collections) for small practices.[1]

PhyCor planned to absorb NAMM's capabilities into its already-existing structure and to offer those services to NAMM clients, ostensibly buying more opportunity to service ever-larger physician populations in the form of a managed services organization (MSO).

PPMs were now consolidating large groups and small practices through direct acquisition or indirectly through purchases like NAMM into a large network of money flow, and then centralizing as much of the flow of money as possible into the MSO.

The MSO served much like a cargo shipping hub (e.g., FedEx or UPS) in which many different practices could drop off claims from all over the country and then pick up a load of payments for return to the practicing physicians. The terminals inside the hub sorted all of the claims, adjudicated the claims, scrubbed the claims, and after taking the 15%, shipped off the cash to its rightful providers.

Doctors were happy in the mid-1990s, as were the PPM and MSO company executives and shareholders. By 1996, Akron Internal Medical Associates was fully engaged with its new PPM capital partner and its scaffolding of its billing/collection partner, the MSO. Gone were the days of physicians employing skilled office managers and teams to manage cash flow. Gone were the contentious payer contract negotiations. Gone, too, would be PhyCor, when in 2002 the company filed for bankruptcy.

THE IRON TRIANGLE OF HEALTHCARE

So, what went wrong? Before we answer that question, be mindful that the splitting of the money was no longer front and center of the physicians in these PPMs. Nor were the contract negotiations. Nor were the inner workings of the billings/collections. The splitting of the money in this era led to a splitting of the work, too, and physicians were finding themselves farther and farther away from the work of claiming their hard-earned fees.

An iron triangle was forming, a relationship denoting a closed mutually beneficial relationship among three stakeholders: physicians, hospitals, and payers. And, at least in theory, if not in outright practice, any improvement to any one side of the triangle invariably caused one of the other two sides to suffer.

LESSONS LEARNED

- Physicians were losing direct authority and negotiating strength over their fees starting with Medicare/Medicaid programs in the mid-1960s, but the impact was not demonstrably felt until commercial plans started to change the playing field in the 1980s.
- Hospitals had more infrastructure and capital to pivot into different models of care delivery despite changes in reimbursements during the same period.

- Private/commercial insurers and physicians began to coalesce into bigger models and structures to achieve more "control" over the money flow.
- "Outside" business structures grew as the volume of administrative services grew to bill and collect the money. These structures became just as complex as the processes themselves (e.g., filing claims, processing claims, adjudicating claims, scrubbing claims, paying claims, etc.).
- There was money to be made in the handling of the money.

QUESTIONS TO ASK

- Where is the CMO in the iron triangle of healthcare today? Where do you want to be? How do you manage the clinical responsibilities when faced with the potential of impacting the other sides of the triangle?
- Should physician fees be the target of healthcare systems? What about facility fees for the care of the patient?
- How can a CMO address the impact of fees on successful operations of the clinical enterprise? As an insurance CMO? As a hospital CMO? Or as a medical group CMO?
- Should a CMO create better systems for fee generation? For fee management? For the sharing of fees? If the answer is "yes," who stands to benefit from better fee management — the physician or the system (e.g., hospital, insurer, group)?
- Where is the responsibility to the patient while managing the fees?

CHAPTER 7

Capitation

"There can be only one captain to a ship."

Dr. Thomas John Barnardo,

Founder of Barnardo's Charity

MIRIAM FISCHER PASSED AWAY from metastatic breast cancer in 1996, after years of battling the disease. She left behind her husband of 29 years, Elias Liontari, and their only child, Sophia, who was halfway through medical school at the Northeast Ohio Medical University at the time. Sophia, or "Sophie" as she was known to her family and close friends, always believed she would end up in the medical field given her exposure to her mother's work, not to mention the years of growing up with Miriam's illness.

At graduation, when Sophie received her medical degree, her father broke down in tears of joy mixed with sadness. Later that night, he experienced crushing substernal chest pain. Sophie took her father to the City Hospital Emergency Department for evaluation. Recall that City Hospital had been progressively building its portfolio of commercial insurance contracts and moving its services to outpatient under HOPD billing to improve its finances.

Sophie was familiar with City Hospital, as she completed several clinical rotations there during her third and fourth years of medical school, most notably in several areas of internal medicine (general medicine, nephrology, critical care, cardiology) and one block in the ED. Recall also that her mother, Miriam, had received chemotherapy and radiation at City Hospital.

When her father was admitted to "rule out MI," she knew all too well how things would unfold. Luckily for the family, Elias was admitted to the medicine service under the newly developed hospitalist program, and his attending physician, Dr. Sam Monroe, was

Sophie's PGY-3 resident at the time of her general medicine rotation. Sophie knew that her father was in good hands.

Elias was diagnosed with a moderate infarction based on his CK and CK-MB enzyme results and was treated with IV streptokinase. He spent several days in the hospital and later underwent cardiac catheterization as part of the workup. During the catheterization, he was found to have two areas of coronary artery stenosis and underwent balloon angioplasty with stenting and, following recent data from France regarding dual anti-platelet therapy, was discharged home on dual anti-platelet therapy, aspirin, and clopidogrel (Plavix).

Elias was discharged home in the care of his sister who had arrived from Pennsylvania to care for him, as Sophie was due to start her internship in Cleveland and could not care for her father without delaying her post-graduate training. Within two weeks, Elias experienced a return of chest pain late at night and his sister called 911 for help.

Elias was taken via ambulance to the nearest facility per EMS protocol: the ED at General Hospital. After the diagnosis of another MI and admission to the floor, Sophie demanded by telephone from Cleveland, as "Dr. Liontari," that Elias be transferred to City Hospital for continuity of care.

Upon Elias's arrival at City Hospital, the admitting intern on the hospitalist service called for medical records for Elias's recent discharge paperwork. Because the chart was still downstairs in coding and billing, it took a couple of days for it to arrive on the ward.

When the records finally arrived, the intern told the medical student on the team to reconcile the discharge medications with the transfer medications from General Hospital. The paperwork from General Hospital included only a brief discharge summary and some papers related to the transfer process.

The medical student had asked Elias for his signature to obtain the ED and admission records from the brief time at General Hospital. When the records were reviewed, the medical student noted there was no mention of clopidogrel anywhere.

When the medical student reported this to his intern, who in turn shared with the resident, attending, and cardiologist, the group concluded that Elias had likely occluded his newly placed stent in part from a lack of adequate anti-platelet therapy. This hypothesis would be further evaluated with a return to the cardiac catheterization lab the next day and, in fact, was proven to be true based on the cardiac catheterization film loop reels.

EXPANDING SERVICE LINES

In the mid-1990s, City Hospital found itself in the midst of a rapid expansion of medical services and stiff competition from its rival hospital, General Hospital, as well as the presence of major health systems located in Cleveland. With the recession of the 1970s and the auto and tire industry downturn long past, the area had seen steady growth in polymer research, finances, software, and other high-tech industries. As such there were many viable employers with strong health plan benefits and the market conditions were competitive at all levels.

Akron's City Hospital had continued to contract with the local HMO, which was holding tight its payment rates to remain competitive regarding premiums for employer benefit packages, and now the hospital elected to invest in a cardiac service line to reap the benefits of high payments for the services.

For about a decade, based on emerging peer-reviewed literature, physicians had become adopters of streptokinase for use in coronary thrombosis. This was not without risk, and careful consideration was given to its administration, but it was also relatively expensive at the time of adoption.

Recall that hospitals no longer received any direct payment for discrete elements of care as they did several decades earlier. If nothing else were to change, then the cost of treating a myocardial infarction would threaten any profitability for any individual case if the patient required the expensive thrombolytic.

With the parallel introduction of balloon angioplasty and shortly thereafter stent placement, any hospital that could perform those invasive procedural services would be also able to bill for the technical component of the procedures and capture more revenue than any prospective payment based on diagnosis alone. And, given the reimbursement rates at the time, even with the cost of IV contrast, catheter devices, balloon equipment, stents, and extra lab staff, the revenues of the procedures exceeded all of the costs.

Paradoxically each and every admission for cardiac care also resulted in, at a minimum, a prospective payment for the care, adjusted of course by the ICD-9 codes, complexity, and acuity. Hospitals benefitted from the high volumes of services and admissions in this service line, even when costs were accounted for.

HOSPITALIST INPATIENT CARE MODEL

City Hospital also was embarking on a new type of inpatient care model, provided by hospitalists, to manage the high volumes of admissions. Dr. Monroe, upon completing his residency, decided that he rather enjoyed the pace of inpatient medicine far more than time spent in an office, and he decided to join the newly created physician-run hospitalist group in Akron.

The group was independent and created its own billing and collection support team, but other than that carried almost no overhead like that of a traditional office or clinic. This naturally allowed them to take home much more of their professional billings as a percentage of their revenue compared to a doctor who carried the overhead of an office (rent, utilities, staff, etc.).

The downside, however, is that there were patients admitted to the hospital who carried no third-party payment coverage and as a result the overall collection percent for a hospitalist was lower than an office-based physician.

This was a tradeoff that was mitigated by attempting to manage as many patients as possible within the hospital and to make up for any non-payments with larger pools of paying patients. Arrangements were loosely crafted for the hospitalists to "take call" for physicians who no longer wanted to visit their patients in the hospital and/or admit from the ED.

The hospitalist group eventually grew large enough and managed enough inpatients that the group and the hospital began to craft an exclusive contract for hospitalist services. For the physicians, this provided protection against any other group entering the facility and disrupting their practice model, and for the hospital the executive team could place stipulations into the contract around length of stay, cost of care, etc., such that patients were managed more efficiently than if left to the independent practitioner who also ran an office.

When Elias was discharged from City Hospital for the second time in less than a month, having suffered two infarctions, unsurprisingly his heart's ejection fraction was believed to be down around 35-40% and he was beginning to show symptoms related to early congestive heart failure. His sister was still his primary caregiver as Sophie was just underway with her internship.

HMOs AND PHARMACY FORMULATIONS

Within a week of the second discharge, this time on clopidogrel and aspirin, Elias had a follow-up with Dr. Staley who had resumed a small clinical practice while also COO for AIMA. By this time, with the national leveraging power of their PPM partner, AIMA now had a contract in place with the HMO in Fairlawn, which coincidentally had shifted from an exclusive internal staff model to a broad community-based network model with more physicians seeing more members.

When Dr. Staley reviewed Elias's recent medical history, given his background at the HMO, he uncovered what had happened after the first discharge, the mystery that had ostensibly eluded the hospitalist team: When Elias was discharged after the first heart attack, his sister dropped off signed prescriptions at the local pharmacy and was told to return the next day to obtain the medications. She followed the instructions and brought home what she was given and thought nothing further of the matter. What she did not know was that the clopidogrel, a brand-new FDA approved product, was not in the bag with the other pill bottles.

When Miriam died, the Fischer-Liontari family was fortunate to remain covered by the HMO insurance plan as part of a death benefit package that was available at that time. This is almost unheard of today but did exist in the late 1980s and early 1990s.

When the clopidogrel prescription was dropped off at the pharmacy, the first thing that the pharmacy had to do was determine what payment it would receive once dispensing the medication. To do that, they had to know if the drug payment was covered under the insurance formulary and how much was covered.

Because the manufacturer's price for the new drug was expensive, the health plan had several opportunities to manage the cost against its bottom line. The health plan created a formulary of products it would cover based on internal discussions and examined clinical best practice, drug equivalencies, substitutions, etc.

Another layer would be to require prior authorization by the prescriber to be sure that the right information would be submitted to establish that the correct drug was being prescribed under the appropriate indications and condition. At the same time, the health plan could make drug coverage contingent on the benefits of the plan itself.

As an example, a health plan could require financial co-pays of the patient as a way of sharing the total cost. In some rare cases, some plans simply did not cover certain medications either because they were too new, or unproven, or to treat a pre-exiting condition that was not covered, or simply not a benefit at all on a very low-cost health plan, regardless of the formulary decision.

Pharmacy benefit management (PBM) companies arose as a result of these complexities. These companies oftentimes, then and now, become the first place the pharmacy contacts to coordinate all of these elements to know if and how much the insurer will pay for the patient's medication.

The PBMs work with the drug manufacturer who also can supply co-pay assistance to patients, by the way, and lower the out-of-pocket expense to the patient. And all of this is done while pharmacies also negotiate with wholesalers for the best pricing when they want to stock up on certain medications that they know will be dispensed.

I will not take readers back to the Hair Salon analogy, as the complexity of this system is way too much for that comparison, but I will suggest they read "Impact of Pharmacy Benefit Managers on Oncology Practices and Patients" in the *JCO Oncology Practice* for a deeper review of this subject.[1]

Suffice to say, this system remains in place today for most commercial/private insurance companies and, in particular, for the management of highly expensive specialty drugs that have entered the healthcare universe in the past 30 years.

Of note, the cost of specialty drugs has continued to grow, totaling $301 billion in 2021, an increase of 43% since 2016. Fewer than 1% of all prescriptions are specialty drugs, but account for 40–50% of total drug spending in 2021.[2] Suffice to say, PBMs on the whole deal with a lot of dollars in today's healthcare climate.

Getting back to Elias's follow-up with Dr. Staley: The physician knew instantly that the pharmacy had sought prior authorization for the brand-new anti-platelet drug, and that either the health plan or the PBM was attempting to secure that from the prescribing physician, who was a hospital-based individual and who had no clinic, office staff, etc., to deal with a prior authorization. So, the prior authorization request sat in limbo. In those days, with the fracturing of hospital-based services and outpatient providers, this was all too common.

Ultimately, after a well-placed phone call by Dr. Staley's office staff to the HMO, and a demand to move the process along through all of the various steps, Elias's sister was able to return to the pharmacy and, with co-pay assistance, pick up the clopidogrel at no out-of-pocket cost to her brother so he could be on the proper treatment quickly.

NATIONAL VERSUS LOCAL FOCUS

Dr. Staley's group had been having quarterly group meetings to review the executive leadership strategies, group finances, and future goals. Recently the group had moved to having them on a monthly basis to tackle two very important issues that had surfaced.

First, AIMA had tried to maintain both the inpatient and outpatient care practices at General Hospital (where there was yet to be a hospitalist service). Second, the Fairlawn HMO contract was up for renewal and contained a new payment model known as capitation.

In 1992, the nation's 600,000 doctors billed more than $200 billion a year, yet they still operated like a cottage industry, with more than three-quarters practicing in groups of fewer than 10.[3] And in the early 1990s, big HMOs were driving down physicians' fees while costs were rising, putting some physicians in "panic mode."[3]

As PhyCor grew, along came MedPartners, another PPM whose original business plan had envisioned a small company with $83 million in annual revenues and 105 physicians under contract after five years of operation. After just one year, the company went public; it took just two years to double its stock, three years to hit the Fortune 500, and four years to top $6 billion in annual revenues.[3] By affiliating with more than 13,000 doctors, MedPartners raced past PhyCor to become the nation's largest PPM.[3]

PhyCor was comfortable slowly buying up large, well-established multispecialty clinics that were the dominant groups in smaller markets, which maximized the company's influence with the giant insurance companies.

The PhyCor approach acknowledged two fundamental realities about the business of medicine: that the patient-doctor relationship remains personal and that the market for medical care is, by its nature, local. By claiming a major share of physicians in a given community and by not signing up large swaths of doctors nationwide, PhyCor believed it would create management efficiencies and leverage with HMOs.

MedPartners, on the other hand, saw itself as a national medical "brand" whose doctors would be sought out by patients across the country wherever they moved or traveled "just as they found comfort pulling into a Midas Muffler shop or Ramada Inn."[3] This concept required getting not just big, but enormous, and the company took aim at 50 major markets across the country.

THE CAPITATION STRATEGY

Coincidentally, California appeared to be leading the nation toward a new approach to the problem of soaring medical costs with a strategy called "global capitation." Capitation pays *the practice* (not the individual physician) a fixed monthly sum to provide care for each insured patient. Thus, if a patient rarely saw a doctor, the practice made a profit on that patient. But if a patient needed a lengthy hospital stay, the practice had to pay the bills and take the loss.

This was similar to Kimball's pre-paid Baylor plan (Chapter 2) in which a lump sum of money (50 cents per teacher, per month) was delivered to the Baylor Hospital and guaranteed 21 days of care per teacher, regardless of the cost of the episode. Baylor Hospital was only "at risk" for care that exceeded the allotted pre-paid 21 days.[4]

Compared to the original Baylor plan, there were two twists in the California physician capitation contracts: (1) the prepaid dollars were sent to the practice as opposed to the hospital, and (2) if a patient cared for by anyone in the practice was hospitalized, the practice paid the hospital bill.

In effect, a capitation contract shifted the financial risk of patient illness from the insurer to the practice, and the practice became a "third-party" payer to the hospital. Each physician in the practice had to be mindful of every care-related decision for the patient and to attempt to lower costs and prevent hospitalizations to hold onto the cash.

Sounds like some sort of hybrid HMO staff model, but in the hands of a "private practice," doesn't it?

For MedPartners, capitation offered potentially huge rewards and equally outsized risks. It guaranteed steady revenue that would grow based on the number of acquired practices and patients. The trick was to minimize expensive procedures and hospital stays. Managing that to ensure a profit is tricky enough at the level of any individual practice; for a big PPM it would be an enormously complex task.

Succeeding at capitation was so difficult and required such finely calibrated management skills that other PPMs ran in the opposite direction when they saw an insurance company armed with a capitation contract.

MedPartners, on the other hand, saw tremendous opportunities and purchased practices in California that were already adept at managing the complex capitation contracts. The rapid growth of the MedPartners portfolio of practices soon dwarfed that of their rival PPM, PhyCor, which threatened the latter's business model. So, the CEO of PhyCor engineered a traditional business response to a threat and announced that PhyCor intended to buy MedPartners.[3]

Tracking the Money

The monthly AIMA group meetings began with a genuine desire to sort out the competing interests of the practice. The PPM operated at a distance in a city hundreds of miles away and had oversight over the types of expenses such as fax machines, carpeting, and staff hiring, but after the 15% was carved out for the PPM, all remaining practice revenue was sent to the physicians. Under the capitation, it became difficult to "split up the money."

When Elias was first hospitalized at City Hospital, every physician involved in his care was paid according to the contract that the HMO had with those doctors. Given that the Fairlawn HMO had moved to a network model, most of those physicians were paid some percentage of the Medicare fee schedule. The attending physician received payments for routine hospital visits, while all the specialists received payments for their hospital visits and their procedures.

In those days, professional payments to cardiologists for cardiac catheterization, balloon angioplasty, and stent placement were substantial and provided a sizable portion of revenue toward their net income.

When Elias was hospitalized a second time and transferred from General Hospital to City Hospital, each physician involved received payment for each and every individual service rendered. But as far as AIMA was concerned, under the newly arranged PPM capitation contract, the practice was now responsible for the payment to City Hospital. Regardless to which hospital Elias was admitted, in fact, AIMA would have been responsible for payment.

It disturbed the AIMA physicians that not only did they have to pay the rival hospital, but because of one "technical" glitch on the part of the pharmacy benefit management team, the practice had to pay for a potentially preventable second admission!

Now imagine if Elias were cared for at AIMA's preferred hospital the first time, General Hospital, and the sequence of care was identical but with only AIMA physicians under the new capitation agreement. How was the group supposed to pay each doctor at the end of the hospital care?

Let's take a look at two cardiologists — the generalist and the interventionalist — involved in a hypothetical admission for Elias at General Hospital. Each physician would be managing several other patients, some under Medicare, some under the Fairlawn HMO, and the remainder split among a variety of private insurers, Medicaid, and no-pay/self-pay.

Each physician, at the end of each day, handed in paper notes to an office manager upon which were recorded the type of care provided (e.g., hospital visit, diagnostic cath, angioplasty, etc.) Those events were converted to charges via a complex process of ICD-9 and CPT coding and submitted to the various payers.

When any charge for a patient whose coverage was provided through capitation was sent to the HMO home office, the claim was scrubbed and no discrete payment was rendered back to the practice, much less assigned to the specific collection bucket of the individual physician who submitted the charge. This was because the money had already been sent to the practice for all of Elias' care that month. Any cardiologists operating in that arrangement would see a significant drop in their personal collections at the end of every month, for all charges for capitated patients were essentially null.

And how should the group split up the capitated payment? Should the group set aside the capitated bucket of money and internally draw from it just like it was any other third party? Well, when they tried it, they found that the amount of capitation money ran out very quickly and there was much less, if any at all, for profitable distribution to the practice physicians in any meaningful way.

The primary care physicians did not mind capitation for several reasons: Their workload demanded less of them and they could certainly see more money at the end of every month, or at least more money for a unit of work. They were also incentivized to avoid hospitalization, which meant they would be far less likely to be awoken at midnight for an admission from the ED.

The procedure-based specialists (e.g., cardiology and gastroenterology), however, were coming up short. Under any fee-for-service model, the proceduralists were assured of income related to their caseload.

Under capitation there was no guarantee of income for the work involved. Even if the cardiologist decided that a procedure was unnecessary and kept the capitated pool of money as high as possible, the share that the physician received ultimately placed his net income lower compared to peers working under fee-for-service.

The Fall of MedPartners

You can imagine the temperature in the room when AIMA physicians began to debate the value of capitation. It literally pitted the physicians against each other. The doctors began to accuse each other of poor medical care and gaming the system. Because they were essentially arguing about the cost of the patient to the practice, they were arguing who should be responsible for the care of the patient, effectively arguing who was "on call."

When PhyCor approached MedPartners for acquisition, there was an intense due-diligence process. PhyCor's due-diligence team immediately found trouble when they first evaluated MedPartners, trouble that grew the more they dug into the finances. The California integration was a joke. The information-management systems were in chaos and thousands of unpaid claims were piled up.

MedPartners had been losing $200 million a year in California alone — the ideal marketplace under capitation! MedPartners closed in 1997 with a net loss of $821 million. Lawsuits from shareholders and physicians began to pile up.[3]

The only area of MedPartners that showed any profit was a little-known subsidiary known as Caremark. In 1992, Baxter International, a powerhouse pharmaceutical business, spun off Caremark which was Baxter's home-infusion subsidiary.[5] For years, there were allegations that Baxter had committed fraudulent billings for its home infusion services. It may be that the spin off from Baxter was part of a negotiated settlement or alternately an attempt to distance Baxter from the looming fraud investigation.

Later, Caremark did several things to diversify. It began to buy and operate rehab hospitals, it began to run PPM services, and it structured a relationship with an Illinois-based company known as Coram in order to operate the ongoing home infusion business.[5]

Caremark/Coram billed insurers for their delivery of services, which was far cheaper than paying for the same service at a hospital-based outpatient infusion clinic, but because the company could do this less expensively than any hospital, they found decent profits in the business. Similar to a staff model HMO, the practice management business could oversee clinical delivery and take a share of the dollars flowing from payers to providers.

For many years, all of the above-named companies were investigated for fraudulent billing, which played its own role in restructuring and legal maneuvers to avoid penalties and impacts to shareholder value. You can read much more about this in *How Health Care in America Became Big Business & Bad Medicine* by two Pulitzer prize winning investigative journalists, Donald Barlett and James Steele.[6]

But germane to this discussion, when MedPartners was liquidated in a fire sale, the former management retained possession of the profitable $2 billion Caremark.[5] Whereas Caremark had started with home infusion following the Baxter spin off, it had quietly and slowly become a major pharmaceutical benefits management company as described earlier in this chapter. You will hear about Caremark again in this book.

In Akron, the AIMA group partners voted to terminate its contract with its PPM capital partner, along with any capitation contracts, and to return to its core business of caring for patients. Given the tenuous legal climate and the fall from grace by MedPartners, the AIMA-PPM termination resolved quickly and without litigation. The physician partners received a hefty payout as a buyback for their vested PPM shares, along with an opportunity to return to fee-for-service contracts. Instead of solving capitation payments, the physicians simply stopped participating.

LESSONS LEARNED

- The splitting of the money in healthcare can be intimately connected to who is actually caring for the patient. Since no single physician can provide 100% of the patient's care over the patient's lifetime, there are a multitude of participants, all of whom are entitled to payment for services rendered.

- Outsourcing the administrative burden of moving the money from payer to provider has positive and negative consequences.
- Physicians are predominately interested in caring for patients, and until and throughout the 1990s, very few physicians had any education, training, or experience in the complexities of payment and money flow.
- Medical information, advanced techniques, and patterns of care rapidly accelerated in the 1990s and this, by its nature, fractured the delivery of care. No longer could citizens simply count on a version of Dr. Puff Ballard to manage all of their care. Pricing of the care became a fluid landscape involving multiple stakeholders, much of which was beyond the skill set of both patient and physician.
- Pricing, costing, and expense management lead to a series of intended and unintended consequences.
- The volume of services became a dominant variable in both cost and revenue areas. There was profit from the management of the cost and the growth of services. A great deal of attention was paid to operational management of the money flow.
- Physicians were slowly losing the vital role in the delivery of the care and may not have entirely understood how to stop that progression.
- Patients were much less in control of their own choices or their own outcomes and became heavily dependent on systems that were out of reach for ordinary people. This is not to say that patients received substandard care, but it appeared that care was taken for granted and occurred with little input from its recipient.
- The physician-patient relationship remained strong, so long as both parties considered the outcome reasonable.

QUESTIONS TO ASK

- As a CMO, do you see the landscape of healthcare as a health *system* or health *market*? A construct designed to produce results or something that is bought and sold? Or all of the above?

- As CMO of a physician group, how aware are you of your physicians' preferences about how they earn a living?

- As CMO of a hospital, how much do you know about the financial stability of the physicians who practice at your facility? How much do you account for their personal incomes? In what ways are you responsible for them?

- As a hospital CMO, are you more responsible for your physicians' financial models or your hospital's/organization's models? Is it "either/or"? Can you insert yourself in either? Both?

- When there are gaps in care (e.g., the medication upon discharge), is that a system fault? An alignment fault? What role does a CMO play, regardless of organizational affiliation (insurer, physician group, hospital)? Do all three bear responsibility for things like a care gap? Who decides? Are you involving yourself in those discussions?

Interlude

By now you might be wondering why you decided to read this book. What does all this history have to do with developing financial aptitude as a chief medical officer in today's environment?

Recall that this book is not an exegesis on finances; rather, is a primer to educate the novice about the basic functions and flows of money in healthcare.

If you wish to be a chief financial officer or possibly a chief executive officer in healthcare, the preparation this book offers will be woefully inadequate. But if you want to establish yourself as a physician executive in your organization, especially a CMO, then allow me to provide you with this interlude to describe some of the key principles and values that are discussed herein.

At the United States' Military Academy, Naval Academy, Air Force Academy, and other military service academies, future officers learn a great deal of military history so they have a framework for higher-order decision-making. This type of leadership development creates foundational context, sharpens critical thinking, and enhances the skill of situational awareness, of understanding why failures occur and where successes materialize.

History also prepares students to take a much longer view than "just in time" thinking. Sometimes, an officer must survey the landscape far and wide to understand the battle, the war, and the long-term peace that is hopefully achieved.

A historical financial review compels a rising CMO to begin to appreciate how patients have been subordinated in the complex system of today's healthcare. How patient care is commoditized, bought, and sold. As such, the financial review should also drive the CMO to visit their own moral compass relative to the purpose of healthcare.

The seeds of today's CMO were planted in the 1990s. As the Health Care Quality Improvement Act (HCQIA) of 1986 coalesced with The Joint Commission on Accreditation of Healthcare Organizations (JCAHO), which was renamed as such in 1987, and

Medical Staff Standards related to peer review were established and revised into the 1990s and early 2000s, hospitals began to assemble physician leaders to share responsibility over traditional medical staff functions.

These early leaders were employed by the hospitals as vice presidents of medical affairs and/or early chief medical officers. The roots of these positions were to ensure that hospitals could uphold the CMS-JCAHO standards around the quality and credentialing of medical staff care delivery.

It was a fairly technical role, but one grounded in the fiduciary responsibility to provide *oversight of the care* delivered by the medical staff. And while the measurable goal was compliance, the broader goal was to ensure the quality and safety of patient care. This is an important example of situational awareness rooted in values, vision, and mission.

In the hectic world of the 1990s–2000s, so much was happening that the next round of physician executive leaders was born more out of necessity than of long-term vision about the care of patients in the organization. And merely 20 years later, financial and regulatory conditions have become more complex, medical knowledge has exponentially increased, and the speed of activities is moving at faster rates than ever before.

ESTABLISHING YOUR COURSE

If you have not already done so, or are open to new perspectives, I encourage you to decide exactly what type of CMO you wish to be. Do you enjoy the technical components of quality, safety, and process improvement? Would you aspire to be a system's senior vice president of quality? Do you prefer to focus on physician care models, hospitalist medicine, emergency medicine, ambulatory environments?

Would you envision leading a large medical group one day, perhaps as a CEO? Are you interested in transformative care delivery that improves the lives of physicians and patients?

Would you see yourself as the system vice president of clinical transformation? Do you want broad scope, broad responsibility, and do you desire to transform entire organizations as the chief clinical officer?

To do any of those things, you must continue to think about the situation in front of you, to evaluate the root causes of issues, to offer interventions and solutions, to consider novel innovative ways to tackle new problems.

You must imagine new payment models with new ways of paying providers, to ensure that value is really added to patient care, to elevate outcomes of health and well-being, and to improve the lives of everyone you serve inside the organization and out. This is a moment to stop and take your own vital signs before leaping forward into the future that awaits you.

CHAPTER 8

wRVUs and RBRVs

"When a man sits with a pretty girl for an hour, it seems
like a minute. But let him sit on a hot stove for a minute
— and it's longer than any hour. That's relativity."

Albert Einstein

DR. SAM MONROE CONTINUED TO WORK at City Hospital and
believed that his independent hospitalist group would continue to
thrive now that it was under an exclusive contract with the hospital.
No other hospitalist group would be able to provide care at City
Hospital under the exclusivity arrangement.

After two years, the hospitalist contract was up for renewal and
Sam was part of the negotiating team that would meet with the
hospital management team consisting of the hospital's COO and
CFO, the same individuals involved in the prior contract negotiation.

Without any prior indication, the hospital invited someone else to
the negotiating table: the COO of a newly formed physician medical
group called Akron Medical Group (AMG). Akron's City Hospital
and AMG had created a partnership under a not-for-profit (shared
services) organization known as Akron City Health, Inc.

Unbeknownst to Sam and his partners, the hospital landscape
continued to be more competitive for the market share of patients in
Akron and surrounding areas. Akron City Health was attempting to
replicate the lucrative services that the hospital had captured within
its cardiac and cancer departments by creating networks of physicians "loyal" to the organization through employment that would
utilize all the available services of the entire organization.

Ultimately, Akron City Health wanted to continue to add even
more services that would also capture more revenue, but it would be
somewhat risky without the appropriate physician base. Also, this
move by the parent company was a defensive maneuver to mitigate
the ongoing strength and growth of the AIMA group, fresh off the

lucrative payout from their PPM shares and their return to their core business. AIMA was now nimbler and more tactical without the interference of the capital partner, much less its MSO functions.

The AIMA leadership decided that its next strategic move was to increase products and services (i.e., revenue) to combat the pressures of maintaining cash flow and to pay for the administrative overhead of billing, scrubbing, and collecting. As such, AIMA announced that it was about to add an outpatient radiation oncology clinic that would directly compete with the Akron City Hospital program.

In a twist of fate, since AIMA was unable to charge the higher hospital-based fees (remember HOPD?), their lower provider-based charges were naturally attractive to the insurance companies, who were always looking to manage costs. And it was not long before AIMA had "cornered" the oncology market, especially when they added an outpatient infusion suite. Several insurance companies no longer enabled easy access to outpatient cancer care at the hospital because they carved out the payments for its beneficiaries who had care provided in the physician-based clinic.

As an aside, in the late 1990s, the quantity of chemotherapeutic drugs that were approved by the FDA created a feeding frenzy of opportunity in community-based, non-hospital oncology services. Non-hospital oncology clinics were reimbursed handsomely at 100% for the cost of the drugs based on a published list of the average wholesale price (AWP) and spun off cash to the practice.[1]

How was this possible? The AWP for a chemotherapy would be listed as $950 and the distributor would "sell" the product to the physician clinic for $1,000, but after bulk discounts and/or rebates, the expense to the clinic might have ended up being only $800. The payment to the clinic was the published AWP ($950), providing a net of $150 into the clinic account after the final expense ($800) of the drug was considered. A "hidden" price structure benefitted the physician's oncology clinic.

SETTING NEW PAYMENT STANDARDS

As the new Medicare fee schedule was rapidly changing (more on that below), an attempt by CMS to more accurately account for payments for chemotherapy met with stiff resistance from the American Society of Clinical Oncology, but CMS was able to set a new standard to pay at 95% of AWP.[1] About a decade later, this was reset to 106% of the *average sales price* (which theoretically was much closer the actual price paid by the clinics), but regardless, oncology clinics continued to see positive cash flow and during this time were allowed to also bill for the drugs and the actual infusion itself, as both were "incident to" the delivery of the care, in addition to the office visit.[1]

To cap it off, this occurred during an explosive growth in the development and utilization of hematopoietic growth factor (e.g., erythropoietin and filgrastim) along with many new and pricey chemotherapies (e.g., paclitaxel), and outpatient oncology clinics found themselves with a sizeable source of cash after expenses.

AIMA was now directly competing with the hospital for a lucrative book of business for both infusions and radiation, with patients appearing to also enjoy the convenience of a clinic model — often felt to be much easier for care than a large hospital environment. As far as AIMA's business imperative, it really was a good unintended consequence rather than a strategic move.

As an aside, this is another example of the "iron triangle." At this time, physician groups were using various strategies (e.g., capital partners, MSOs, Medicare payments) to strengthen their operations; these had direct impacts on hospitals and, in some cases, were an unintended benefit for the insurance company.

But Sam was just a principled leader in the hospitalist group and, because he was still rather early in his career, had no real understanding of all of these moving pieces. So, when AMG offered to buy the hospitalist service, he was both surprised and unprepared. AMG made a very particular offer, too. They offered two components: (1) to pay each physician 10% more than they were earning presently, and (2) to pay going forward *based on charges*, for all patients, regardless of their ability to pay!

When Sam took this back to the group for discussion, imagine their delight when the math showed that their income might go up 15–20%! No longer would they have to chase self-pay or poorly paying third parties. The income was guaranteed!

Of course, when Sam met with the Akron City Health team again, he, along with his peers, were very interested in hearing more about the payment structure.

BEYOND CUSTOMARY, PREVAILING, AND REASONABLE

Recall that when Medicare began, physicians were charging "usual and customary and reasonable" fees, but as things unfolded in the early 1980s, CMS, the AMA, and the physicians adopted a similar phrase to denote fees: "customary, prevailing, and reasonable" (CPR) charges.[2]

Note the word *prevailing*, which is not a trivial term and would foretell a fundamental shift in physician payments forever. Medicare defined *customary* charges as the median of an individual physician's charges for a specific service during a defined time period. The *prevailing* charge for this service was set at the 90th percentile of the customary charges of all peer physicians in a defined region.[2] As you can imagine, there would be tremendous variation in the payments across the U.S.

To make matters worse, in an effort to control Medicare spending (remember there were more people and more services to pay for than initially imagined), the government put two cost containment measures in place. The first was to lower the prevailing charge from the 90th percentile to the 75th percentile and the second was to enact a freeze on payment rates.[2]

In 1976, the freeze was lifted; however, any increase going forward was tied to the general economy, known as the Medicare Economic Index, or MEI. And even as innovations in clinical practice and technology spread geographically, the payment pattern was so "fixed" that charge patterns that prevailed during the 1970s remained in place until a change occurred in 1992.[2]

Naturally, physicians pushed back for years at the MEI-based model, and with the support of the AMA, a new model was evaluated and put into place based on a notion of "relative values" developed years earlier in California.

As we saw before, the change in the payment model began as a local initiative before any widespread adoption. The California

Medical Association (CMA) developed the first relative value scale (RVS) for charges in 1956 and it was based on median charges reported by California Blue Shield. Physicians in that state, correspondingly, used the RVS *to* set their own fee schedules, and subsequently several California state Medicaid programs, Blue Cross/Blue Shield plans, and commercial insurers used it to establish physician payment rates.[2]

Note that in this context, fees were the basis of the scale, which payers used to set payments, and the CMA attempted to update each iteration to create a value-based scale for the service rendered. The process was intimately connected through this circuitous reflection of fees and payments, and organized medicine (CMA) acted as an intermediary to bring some objectivity and restraint into this circular flow of money.

What was unique about this process was the use of a scale to place payments on a spreadsheet relative to each payment's value regarding the service. Naturally, when compared to each other, some payments would have more "value" than others.

Over time, though, interest grew in moving from purely *charge-based* relative values to *resource-based* values. As the expense of resources (e.g., office overhead) increased, the physician demanded that the payments take the rising overhead into account.

A RESOURCE-BASED PAYMENT MODEL

After several years of contentious debates wherein most stakeholders began to agree that any model that is based purely on charges (frozen or otherwise) would continuously be distorted by regional differences, specialty differences, and expense differences to name a few, there was tacit consensus to further investigate a resource-based model instead.

In a rather odd twist, Congress, under pressure to contain overall Medicare spending as well as pressure from the AMA and others to specifically address physician fees, agreed to embark on an ambitious plan to re-structure the Medicare physician fee methodology.

Using ongoing work performed by Harvard, the newly formed Physician Payment Review Commission (PPRC) evaluated in 1986 what a resource-based relative value (RBRV) scale would look like.[2] With comprehensive data across multiple specialties obtained from the Harvard data, the commission initially looked at only two resource items — time and complexity of the service — but over the course of several years and at the urging of the AMA, the PPRC also evaluated the physician practice cost and the cost of liability insurance.

Subsequently, a plan to enact a resource-based payment model was formed and the transition to Medicare's RBRV-based physician payment system began in 1992 and was fully implemented in 1996, culminating nearly a decade of effort by the medical profession and the government to change the way Medicare pays for physicians' services.[2] And it wasn't long thereafter that the RBRV scale was joined to something known as the relative value unit (RVU).

THE RVU CONSTRUCT

When Sam, along with his hospitalist partners, returned to negotiate with Akron City Health, they learned that the organization proposed an employment contract wherein the physicians would be paid a base salary of an amount equal to their current income plus 10% and a fixed dollar amount per work relative value unit ($/wRVU) beyond their current work productivity.

The RVU construct took the hospitalists by surprise on many levels. This was not a model they were expecting nor did they understand it. The physicians fully expected to be paid 100% based on charges, regardless of payment, collections, etc. That was how they interpreted their earlier discussions with Akron City Health. The administrative team realized their misstatements and explained their proposal.

When the RBRV Medicare fee schedule was implemented, it created a new method of establishing the basis for *any fee for any service*. What was poorly understood at the time was that along with the fee analysis, CMS also created the RVU, a unit measurement for any service; every CPT code for every service could be rendered into an RVU. With that construct, every activity of a physician was now accounted for in units rather than fees.

Further, there are three discrete components that factor into today's RVUs: (1) the physician work/activity, (2) the practice expense (added in 1999) that supports that work, and (3) the professional liability insurance surrounding the work (added in 2000).[3]

If you compare a routine office visit for sinus congestion to a craniotomy, for example, it's clear that the work, cost, and liability are quite different between the two clinical scenarios. As such, let's imagine that the RVU for an office visit to evaluate sinus congestion (CPT 99213) is 2.68 while the craniotomy (CPT 61510) is 66. That seems to be logical and rational knowing what is involved with both services.

In addition to the RBRV and the RVU, CMS also established the CMS "conversion factor," which is the dollar amount that is multiplied by the RVU to establish what the payment will be. So, in the above model, if the conversion factor is $33.00, then the office visit will be paid at $88.44 (2.68 × $33) while the craniotomy will be paid at $2,178 (66 × $33).

The conversion factor (CF) is updated every year to include the MEI, an expenditure target (performance adjustment), and budget neutrality, which is a little-known piece of the very same legislation that created the RBRV scale (the Omnibus Budget Reconciliation Act of 1989).[2,4]

Budget neutrality as it pertains to CMS mandates that any estimated increases of $20 million or more to the Medicare physician payment schedule — created by upward payment adjustments or the addition of new procedures or services — must be offset by cuts elsewhere,[3] meaning, in essence, a zero-sum game for all physicians participating in Medicare fee payments.[3]

The entire pool of money available to those physicians is relatively static, forcing a whole lot of "splitting of the money" to occur without any one individual physician's influence on the matter. Of note, Congress can (and often does) legislate additional funding to CMS to add more money to the pool to pay more money; however, this has been challenging politically and is likely unsustainable at some point.

Akron City Health explained to Sam that if he were earning about $250,000/year and if he were generating about 4,000 wRVUs, he could expect to be paid about $62 per wRVU. He would hand in his daily charges for rounding on his hospital patients and each charge would be converted to a wRVU. He would be paid an additional $62 per wRVU over his baseline 4,000 total wRVUs. As the new employer, Akron City Medical Group would cover all of the expenses of the practice, including the billing, collecting, and medical malpractice insurance costs.

After the discussions were held at Akron City Health's corporate headquarters, the physicians returned to their small office across the street from the hospital and began to explore the proposal. When they noted that the CF posted by CMS that year was $33, they were immediately confused and even suspicious of the hospital. The physicians looked up the RVU for a routine follow-up visit and found that it was 2.68. They multiplied that by $33 and determined a payment to the hospital system was $88.44.

They called Akron City Health's CFO the next day and asked for an explanation. The CFO told them that for an average follow-up visit worth 2.68 RVUs, indeed the hospital should receive $88.64 for a Medicare patient, but the physicians must remember that the new employer would be paying for all of the office expenses (billing and collecting) as well as each physician's medical malpractice, hence the $26 difference ($88-$62). The CFO also reminded the doctors that they would still be paid for each wRVU regardless of the patient's insurance or ability to pay.

After huddling again, the doctors countered with a request for $65 for each wRVU for Medicare patients, but $85 for each non-Medicare patient. The CFO again politely pointed out that there was no way to pay that much for the under-insured/self-insured/non-insured patients, at least not without potentially running afoul of the fair market valuations (FMV) for physician compensation as per the recently enacted Stark Law.[5]

Under FMV, physician arrangements must meet one or more of three requirements: (1) that the arrangement be commercially reasonable, (2) that the amounts paid not be based on the "volume or value of referrals or other business generated for a party," and (3) that the amounts paid be consistent with fair market value.[5]

Sam spent many days and nights mulling this over with his part-ners. On the one hand, they would be guaranteed payment; on the other hand, they felt that they were somehow getting a raw deal.

As part of the next steps in the negotiation, Akron City Health asked for the physicians' historical billings. With that information, they would be able to predict the physicians' income more accurately by converting all of their prior charges to wRVUs and calculating what their anticipated future earnings would be at $62/wRVU. This would be part of the due diligence of acquisition and would be important from a valuation perspective, especially to determine if the group would be paid in accordance with FMV and both parties would remain clear of any Stark Law violation.

After all parties agreed in writing to allow this exchange of infor-mation, the results were shared with the physicians. The proposal appeared more than fair and suggested that the physicians were indeed better off under the employment model even at the proposed $/wRVU.

When the hospitalists received the formal term sheet for the acquisition outlining everything that was agreed upon, they met again to debate the sale. The opinions were as wide as the ocean, and not unlike those expressed by AIMA when it was considering the role of a PPM.

Some of the physicians were upset about becoming hired labor, sharing that their value was reduced to a wage for their work (and further reduced to discrete units of work). They feared the wage was somewhat of a fixed price, since they would be paid based on CMS tabulations for all patients, including those who carried commercial, employer-based insurance, which paid much higher.

They feared that they would lose any autonomy on how hard they would work and for how much. They feared that if the Medical Group did not want to renew the contract in the future, they might not survive. Would they be unable to re-structure and practice at the hospital or would they fall victim to an exclusive arrangement with another hospital group?

Some in the group had a real sense of paranoia; for others it was more about pragmatism. Overall, however, there was emotional turbulence around issues of pride, self-worth, control, etc.

Sam, however, was at peace, comfortable with the outsourcing of all the requirements of being in a private practice (albeit hospital based) to focus on patient care. He did not see the situation exactly in the same way as his partners, but in the end, despite each individual's level of comfort with the arrangement, the group unanimously agreed to the contract terms.

As for the newly formed Akron City Health company, they saw an opportunity to further operationalize all of the hospital-based services with the addition of hospitalists to its infrastructure. They believed they would be able to collect the physician fees, pay for all of the physician expenses, efficiently and effectively deliver a variety of care services, and reap the benefits of such an arrangement. They, too, were at peace.

LESSONS LEARNED

- The creation of a scale (RBRV) to determine a physician's payment was another tectonic shift in the marketplace of medical care. The irony is that the new scale had its origin in arbitrary (usual and customary) fees that had simply evolved over time without any real economic value assigned to the service provided. Before Medicare, hospitals billed for specific items with a markup, but physician's fees were arbitrary at best. This begs the questions: How does one determine a fee for the ability to evaluate a patient and render a diagnosis? How do you quantify that skill? How do you differentiate a fee for cutting into the peritoneum versus the thorax?

- The creation of RVUs could easily be seen as a way of determining what is inherent in the nature of a service as labeled by a CPT code. An office visit requires a certain amount of cognitive work, has office expenses associated with that, and carries a burden of liability, but there is no true standard at work; rather it is essentially modeled after a traditional distribution (bell) curve across a large data set. Some physicians can accomplish an office visit quickly, some slowly, and sometimes with help (i.e., extra expense). Sometimes the patient simply takes longer to see regardless of physician style or support.

- The origins of RBRVs and RVUs are based on historical factors across a wide range of services and locations. By nature, some fees will end up being "winners" and some being "losers."

- The formula of payment used by CMS, which in turn becomes the benchmark for most, if not all, insurers, is that today's Medicare physician payment is equal to the RVU × the CF. It is as if, in a twist of fate, the fees of the 1970s created the fees of today since all of the RBRVs and the RVUs were created from all of the prevailing charges of days gone by.

- Even more ironic, the CF as a benchmark could only have been derived from all of those payments. Had the payments been set at 110% of prevailing, for example, the CF would have to be higher to arrive at the "right" payment.

- Any physician or medical group on a physician's behalf who bills CMS is paid under the RBRV-RVU-CF construct. The AMA has copyrighted the CPT codes and the datasets that allow any physician to convert their CPT based charges into RVUs. The AMA charges for access to those conversion tables.

- The practice expense is 45% of every RVU; so, if a payment of $100 is made to the physician who manages his own practice, if his office overhead expense is less than 45% of total collections, then any difference is essentially captured and returned to the physician income. In hospital settings, it is highly unlikely that overhead is less than 45%, so, in fact, large physician employers are likely unable to pay the remaining 55% to the physician. And, if they do, they will be making up those dollars somewhere else in the system.

QUESTIONS TO ASK

- When working with employed physicians, whether hospital based or ambulatory, should the CMO be involved in how those physicians be paid? Why or why not?

- Should a CMO who oversees employed physicians have influence over the $/wRVU? Or any other methodology? Who sets the standards of expected work output? What about quality and safety? Is that compensable?
- Can a CMO be balanced if some of the physicians are employed by the system and fall under his/her scope, while others are independent practitioners? How does one maintain credibility and integrity under a hybrid environment?
- Do hospitals truly benefit from having employed physicians? How do you know that? How could you determine that? How does the CMO engage on that topic?
- Should hospitals share their positive margins with employed physicians? Is that permissible? Are there avenues to explore in this regard? Should CMOs advocate for this? What happens if hospitals lose money? Is this also true in ambulatory clinic settings?
- Should a CMO align patient quality, safety, and outcomes to physician income when the current basis for payment is all about the quantity of work performed? If so, how? What tools are at the disposal of the CMO?
- Why do wRVUs focus on the "work" rather than the outcome?
- Should physicians be paid simply to "work"? Is the wRVU system devaluing physicians? Is it fair for patients that their physicians are incentivized to work? Rather than incentivized to produce best outcomes?
- When physicians (or patients) argue that the system seems so unfair and messy, what is your response?

CHAPTER 9

Meaningful Use/EHR

"Say what you mean and mean what you say."
Gen. George S. Patton, Jr.

WHEN DR. SOPHIA LIONTARI FINISHED her residency in Cleveland, she packed up her belongings (of which there were few) and drove down Interstate 77 into South Carolina. With a short diversion to pick up I-95, she made her way to Jacksonville, Florida. She had no close family ties in Ohio after her father's death from congestive heart failure at the beginning of her third year of post-graduate training.

She had searched for a variety of practice opportunities that would allow her to be a private practitioner, but not require any inpatient responsibilities. While she enjoyed hospital-based care, she ultimately wanted to raise a family and believed that a role centered around an office schedule would best accommodate her plans.

The opportunity that seemed most inviting involved a large multispecialty practice in Jacksonville that had ties to a hospitalist group and had survived the PPM era unscathed. It boasted almost 130 physicians along with a large number of advanced practitioners (nurse practitioners and physician assistants) and had over 35 years of experience in the area.

When she settled in and began to work at the practice, she found herself rather at ease. The abundant sunshine always brightened the mood and everyone seemed happy at the clinic. There were plentiful patients to be seen, as Florida was a growing state with a great mix of the elderly and young people in the surrounding metropolitan area.

Sophie fell in love with an electrophysiology cardiologist, married him, and had two children. In the aftermath of September 11, 2001, and with the naval station in Jacksonville, there was a powerful sense of pride and patriotism just about everywhere Sophie turned.

She enjoyed the collegiality of her peers, found a balance between her work and her family, and, most of all, enjoyed a tremendous amount of latitude to practice medicine in all of the ways that she imagined it was supposed to be.

With national attention diverted to the "war on terror," Washington policymakers were not devoting as much attention to the delivery of U.S. healthcare between 1994 and 2004, aside from the launch of the Health Insurance Portability and Accountability Act (HIPAA) in 1996 which, among other things, restricted the consideration of pre-existing conditions in health insurance coverage determinations.[1]

The only other significant changes were two outcomes of the 1997 Balanced Budget Act, which established the Medicare + Choice program (expanding Medicare options in the HMO and other commercial insurance spaces and named Medicare Advantage in 2003) and changes in provider payments to slow the growth in Medicare spending.[1]

For Sophie, that meant even more insured patients since they could no longer be denied coverage based on pre-existing conditions, and better collections for those elderly in Medicare + Choice, compared to elderly patients who lacked any supplemental coverage (or personal ability to pay) for office-based care.

These additional sources of revenue generally seemed to offset any decrement in payment of the Medicare fees, at least as far as Sophie could tell. Her medical group had a large file room in the administration office and Sophie could track her daily charges, collections, and outstanding A/R on large printouts spit out by an old dot matrix printer.

At the end of every month, the financial committee met to review the monthly finances and to send recommendations to the group's board (made up entirely of physicians) about profit sharing (i.e., splitting) of any excess cash collected from its various ancillary services.

It was Sophie's husband who first noticed a widening gap in his charges and his collections…but more on that later. If her husband was able to come home in time to have dinner with her and the children, they might chat about a variety of matters but oftentimes not about the "business" of the practice.

Sophie made a point of finishing every paper chart note and returning all phone calls at the end of her clinic hours every day so she could be home for dinner every night. Sometimes the charts were misplaced in the file room (which was adjacent to the film library and reading room) and she might try to retrieve them on their own and/or look at chest x-rays that she ordered just to corroborate the radiologist report.

These brief moments among the charts or the film jackets brought her back to her days of medical school and training when she was tasked with collecting those items for her senior residents and providing her best differential diagnosis with the information in hand. Regardless, she now rather enjoyed the autonomy of private practice and that more often than not, someone else was bringing the films and charts to her.

THE CONVERSION TO THE
ELECTRONIC HEALTH RECORD

In 2004, President George W. Bush declared his vision of an electronic health record (EHR) for everyone within 10 years. Through the Health Information Technology for Economic and Clinical Health (HITECH) Act of 2009, Congress provided $27 billion to eligible professionals (EPs) and hospitals that adopted health IT and used it to improve care delivery under the Medicare or Medicaid programs.[2]

What was striking in retrospect, but again not surprising, was that the U.S. government created a series of requirements around the EHR for the healthcare user to obtain any of the available funding. In other words, there was a pool of money to be shared, so long as the swimmers knew how to play by the pool rules.

Simply adopting and using a technology system would not suffice as adequate criteria to receive the federal funding. The use of any EHR would have to satisfy the requirements of meaningful use (MU) of health information before any federal payments were made to a hospital or a medical professional.[2]

Further, a timeline allowed for a gradual adoption of such technologies, and there was even an incentive from 2011 until 2014, but after that, a penalty for *not* adopting in the form of decreasing payments by Medicare.[2]

Even more striking than rules of participation in the conversion to an EHR was the relationship between the nation's largest payer and the practitioners. Essentially, CMS was now directly shaping the practice environment and either rewarding or penalizing the adoption of such an environment.

If one of the key economic forces at work in modern healthcare is the expense of the practice, then it was largely without precedent that a payer was attempting to actually define the practice ecosystem.

Ins and Outs of Adoption

The discussions at AIMA and at Akron City Health, as well as at Jacksonville Medical, Inc. (JMED) where Sophie and her husband worked, were all roughly the same. The respective groups' financial planners evaluated the cost of adopting a computer-based health record system (hardware acquisition price, software purchase price, license fees and annual renewals, conduits, cabling, wiring, etc.) against the financial benefit (short-term incentives and/or bumps in payments) and the potential penalty for non-adoption.

Some physicians were naturally what leadership expert Malcolm Gladwell calls "early adopters" and had already been clamoring for a better system rather than continuing to rely upon oftentimes lost and missing paper charts, with paper notes, imaging reports, and lab results.[3]

Others were uninterested in using any form of computerized record keeping because paper always worked fine for them and they lacked the desire to learn any new skill (e.g., typing or transcribing).

A small number of more senior physicians were quietly demoralized and deflated at the notion that there was going to be any interference at all about how to practice medicine, that anyone, much less the U.S. government, had any influence on how physician ran their office infrastructure. Those quiet few were quickly outnumbered by the larger number of voices that advocated for adoption and the financial upside, while an equal number were much less willing to incur any financial downfall if the group(s) failed to adopt this new tool.

Tracking Quality Measures

To qualify for financial incentives, HITECH required physician offices and hospitals to demonstrate effective use of *certified technology*, to engage in *information exchange*, and to report on *quality measures* as specified by the U.S. Department of Health and Human Services (HHS).[2]

And, for the first time since CMS and other payers had required a system of coding and documentation to process claims (and all of the incumbent costs associated as described in Chapter 4), physicians and hospitals were now required to send data on certain quality measures.

Briefly, some early adopters believed that this would truly be transformative to the clinical care of patients, as quality data could conceivably be used to improve patient outcomes. They were quickly disappointed, however, as the objectives and measures were generally process measurements rather than health outcomes. (CMS has a description of these elements on its website.[4])

By way of example for our purposes, some of the objectives/measurements include the following: use of computerized provider order entry of medication (30% of patients have at least one medication ordered electronically by provider), electronic prescribing (eRx) (40% of prescriptions are transmitted electronically to the pharmacies), and clinical summaries for patients (50% of all visits provided to patients within three days).[4]

Notably, these goals were for Medicare beneficiaries, but functionally this created a workflow constraint on most practitioners and forced the practice to have a way to segregate Medicare beneficiaries from all other patients electronically and to collect, collate, and report those elements accordingly.

Once more, we have a system that is adding financial motivation and financial expenses, including physical equipment and more managerial staff in the form of IT leadership, infrastructure, and informatics.

THE IMPACT ON DAILY WORK

In large, nimble, forward-facing practices such as AIMA or JMED, the executive physician leaders saw an opportunity to transition the file room staff into informaticists and/or IT support to keep the conversion cost neutral and to avoid hiring too many more individuals. Smaller practices were simply ill-equipped at first to add all of this to their pipeline, while hospitals and bigger systems were too bureaucratic to do this quickly and without disruption.

Needless to say, everyone in healthcare felt this next tectonic shift, but most acutely and more so than with the prior two (billing/collection and the creation of RVUs), physicians felt the earth move under their feet. The implementation of MU and an EHR had a physical impact on the physician's daily workflow and activity.

The other shifts occurred in administrative hallways and in workflows by a hidden workforce involved in billing and finance. For those attempting to adopt an EHR, especially to meet the MU standards, this one occurred with each and every Medicare patient encounter both inside the hospital and out and required a new set of steps in patient care. These steps were not exactly for the patient's health or outcome, much less to provide a "better" document to use for patient care. Nobody in medical school was trained to use the computer in this way as part of their workflow.

For these new requirements to be accomplished and for the practice to see a better reimbursement from the $27 billion government allocation, many more tasks were added to the physician's work. And, correspondingly, *there was no increase in the work component of the RVU*. There was no increase in "value" of time in the calculation of payment to the physician, even though the time had increased, at least compared to the days of paper workflows. The EHR required more data entry, data capture, more steps, etc.

On average, for every hour of direct patient care, a physician spends two hours working in an EHR.[5] Until a position paper appeared in 2019 arguing that this was woefully and inadequately captured in CMS's payments, physicians had been spending a portion of their time on activities that are not adequately reimbursed.

Note that until now, I have presented to you that physicians have been paid a fee, no matter how derived, for the cognitive and/or procedural skill that they acquired in medical school and in residency. Consider this concept more deeply as you contemplate your CMO aspirations and as you continue to read this primer.

As we discussed briefly early on in the book, if health is a commodity that can be bought and sold, we must begin to determine what the system is buying and selling today and in what form. Is it the skill? Is it the outcome? Is it the time involved? Is it something else?

Not all practices adopted EHR and participated in MU, although most hospitals did.[6,7] Some scrappy practices undoubtedly calculated that the amount of time spent working within an EHR was not worth any incentive payments (that eventually dried up after 2015) or any ongoing penalty for non-adoption.

As an example, if you were a solo practitioner or you could be singly attributed your "meaningful use" in a group practice, you could receive $44,000 over five years (2011–2015) if you adopted early and attested to all of the objectives and measures every year during that period. That is an average of $8,800 per year. How many hours per year would be required to obtain the average payment of $8,800?

Any physician who calculates their time as a value expressed in dollars might deduce that spending time working in the EHR (not to mention time spent on training, overseeing, implementing, etc.) was a losing proposition. Spending just one extra hour per day in a new EHR would be five hours/week, and if the physician worked 48 weeks (taking four weeks of vacation), that amounts to 240 hours/year. If we calculated that as a wage, ($8,800/year divided by 240 hours/year), it amounts to $36/hour — and that is based on a conservative estimate of time spent within the EHR.

If an average physician conservatively estimates that she earns (after all overhead expenses) $100/hour and if the extra five hours/

week, rather than being consumed in an EHR, were compensated at that rate, that would amount to almost $24,000.

MEDICAL INFORMATICS AS AN INDUSTRY

While physicians (and hospitals) were facing this new reality, the infusion of $27 billion created a new industry (or bolstered a nascent one) in the form of medical informatics. Just as an industry grew up around billing, coding, scrubbing, and collecting, the same held true for medical informatics.

Large companies, some who had a footprint in medical devices and care delivery, began to establish new ventures and diversify into medical informatics. General Electric spawned GE Health, originating in the manufacturing of X-ray tubes and subsequent imaging devices such as CT and MRI scanners, which in turn acquired MedicaLogic, creator of the former Logician, an ambulatory electronic medical records system, and Millbrook Corporation, maker of Millbrook Practice Manager, a billing and scheduling system for doctors' offices.

GE would later merge the two products into one and create EHRs for sale to its customer base in both the inpatient and outpatient arena.[8,9] One of their products, known as Centricity, became a viable option for large medical groups.

To acquire the platform and all of its hardware components, practices would have to create a new overhead expense in their budgeting meetings. This would cause both an immediate need for capital and a budget for ongoing expenses, but would not be reimbursable in the same way as adding laboratory or imaging services. This was, therefore, another "cost of doing business" for which there was no immediate or direct payment, so it became another overhead allocation which, in turn, took more money out of the bottom line for the physicians, the hospital, or the shareholders.

THE NEED FOR INTEROPERABILITY

CMS continued to refine the steps toward ongoing implementation of an EHR and moved toward additional responsibilities such as interoperability as a strategy to create more efficiency in the informatics arena.

When MU was initiated, the products that flooded the health-care delivery systems already had multiple computerized systems in place and none of them were designed for a holistic EHR or vice versa. These various components could not "talk" to each other and required ongoing work from informaticists and IT specialists to build software and networks to create some type of interoperability.

Similarly, CMS wanted to encourage systems to talk with each other not just within the hospital or clinic walls, but to outside entities such as pharmacies, nursing homes, rehab hospitals, etc. All of this cost, time, money, and labor further strained the available resources of the key stakeholders.

The $27 billion could easily be characterized by an observer as a bloated infusion of cash into an already disparate system, making it even more clunky and, possibly, if not borne out by time and events over the past decade, as a tremendous wedge between who is spending time on call for the patient and how the money is being split.

If you have not yet begun to develop an increasing situational awareness that you will find yourself in as a CMO, this would be a good opportunity to re-consider your decisions and/or to refine what exactly you most prefer about being a physician executive. The situation will never get any simpler, at least for the foreseeable future, but with your growing awareness, you may be equipped with new skills by which you can transform your role and/or those organizations and the people you serve.

QUESTIONING MEANINGFUL USE

Sophie's medical group, known as JMED, decided to adopt an EHR and to do it quickly to maximize the incentives. After an intense review of available products and pricing, and after selection and acquisition, the practice devoted a significant amount of time and resources to launching their EHR and to meet every objective and measure in each stage of adoption as determined by CMS.

Sophie found herself falling behind each day while in the office. She seemed unable to keep pace with the patient schedule and to multitask the entries into the computer or do it effectively at the end of the day. On some days, especially if there were a lot of physicians in clinic, or if the EHR was going through an upgrade, the system would slow down and she would have to wait or, if logged out, would wait interminably to log back in.

She was not alone, and several physicians asked for the IT staff to accommodate access to the EHR at night on their home PC. The same system slowness occurred at home as well for several reasons, two of which were scheduled downtime and/or maintenance for data management or other bug fixes, preferably to be done during the least-busy times of system use when the offices were closed.

Sophie and her husband no longer could synchronize their dinner time given her chronic lateness in completing work at the office. Their time together later at night when the kids were asleep was interrupted when she brought home "work" to be done on the home PC. At the same time, her husband was increasingly more concerned about how busy he was, too, and no longer seemed to be able to generate the same amount of income as he had five years earlier.

Meaningful use was neither meaningful nor useful to either of them.

LESSONS LEARNED

- As medical complexity grew, new systems were developed to manage an overwhelming amount of data and information. Ideally, electronic systems should be built to produce effective data management and improve outcomes.
- Influence into a system comes in many forms and new structures can appear strategic at first glance, but may, in fact, be something quite different once implemented.
- Increased work does not always come with increased reward. In the case of MU/EHR adoption, for outpatient practices the renumeration was low per hour of work and at some point, no longer had any positive revenue.
- The requirement to adopt an EHR appeared inescapable; however, the strategic elements to manage this were often myopic and mismanaged.

- The U.S. government was shaping the architecture of medical practice and, in parallel, large companies were making moves into this intersection of medical care and the micro-environment of care delivery.
- In September 2005, GE HealthCare acquired IDX Systems Corporation, a leading healthcare information technology provider, for $1.2 billion and renamed itself GE HealthCare Integrated IT Solutions, specializing in clinical information systems *and* healthcare revenue management.[10]
- The GE HealthCare Integrated IT Solutions was later shaped into Virence, but still managed its EHR, known as Centricity.
- In parallel, athenahealth, a healthcare technology and services company, was also creating an EHR, and in 2020 merged with Virence in a $5.7 billion deal, with a new series of products, including cloud-based EHR/revenue cycle management solutions, named athenaIDX, a nod to its history tied to GE.[11]

QUESTIONS TO ASK

- Should a CMO be involved in the decisions involving physician workload, particularly if it involves increasing tasks? Why or why not? Should there be renumeration for increasing work? Why or why not?
- Could a CMO articulate an argument that extra work should equate with extra pay? Does extra work also equate to increasing overhead requirements? Who should shoulder the costs of new workflows?
- Could a CMO design a method to appropriately allocate funds when work increases?
- Should healthcare "pay for" extra work? Does that continue the upward cycle of rising overall costs? Does this just incentivize more work?
- Are there any other ways to incentivize physicians other than money? Or is that the best way to change physician behavior?

- Are physicians able to work at the "top of their license" in your system? Who else can do certain tasks and at what cost to free up physician skill delivery?
- While CMOs may be positioned to imagine workflows, top of license work, and appropriate payment, recognize that your IT departments, CMIO colleagues, CIO colleagues, and your CEO are bracing themselves against IT companies that can grow 5x in valuations. How do you hold your position and have those conversations with those peers? Do you have situational awareness of the macroenvironment?

CHAPTER 10

Hospitals — Part 2

"You know, 97% of the time, if you come into
a hospital, everything goes well. But 3% of
the time we have major complications."

Atul Gawande, MD, MPH

DR. KEVIN J. RAMSEY, the EP cardiologist married to Sophie, was
approached by the hospital's director of the cardiac service line to
consider taking on a project to reduce the number of patients diagnosed with congestive heart failure who were re-admitted within 30
days of an initial hospitalization.

Kevin was unaware that this was an issue and uncertain why he
was selected for the project. He did not directly treat that patient
population, nor did he want to spend time doing administrative work.

After more than a week considering the request, he finally spoke
to Sophie about it late one evening. She listened carefully and then
told him that the medical director of the hospitalist team had mentioned during a recent lunch "update" meeting with the physicians,
that the hospital was going to be penalized if it did not better manage six conditions that each incurred a variable, but unacceptable,
number of readmissions.

As we have discussed, hospitals were paid on a DRG (prospective) basis for medical conditions such as CHF and were paid each
time patients were admitted, regardless of how many times this
might occur, even within a few days or weeks of the previous admission. Like meaningful use and EHR implementation, CMS was once
again going to change the payment structure to incentivize a change
in the model of care delivery, but this time focused within the hospital's clinical environment.

The hospitalists were put on notice that they, too, would be held
accountable for their individual "bounce backs" related to CHF.
None of them were particularly happy about these directives because,

as hospital-based physicians, they knew that they were only responsible for what happens to a patient from the time the admission is requested in the ED until the discharge, and many readmissions are related to a host of variables outside of the hospital walls.

Beginning with the Affordable Care Act in 2010, legislation required CMS to implement something called value-based payments (VBPs) across several domains, including inpatient care.[1] CMS described VBP as "part of our larger quality strategy to reform how health care is delivered and paid for."[2] The VBP programs support the notion of delivering the right care at the right time, and for lower cost.

One of the earliest VBP programs was the Hospital Readmission Reduction Program (HRRP), established to do exactly as its name suggests.[3] The original intent was to focus on quality outcomes rather than rewarding the quantity of services. The HRRP was phased in over several years and ultimately could reduce a hospital's base operating payment from CMS by up to 3% in 2015.[3]

Another program was the Hospital-Acquired Condition Payment Reduction, which, beginning in 2015, could reduce payments to acute care hospitals based on their performance on select risk-adjusted hospital-acquired condition (HAC) quality measures.[3] The top 25% worst performing hospitals would receive a payment reduction of 1% for all discharges in those hospitals.[3]

As most readers are likely familiar with these concepts and perhaps have even been involved in their facility's workflows to deal with the clinical outcomes that impact payment to the hospital, we will not dive into the inner workings of these payment models. If you would like to review them, you can find them online.[3]

Back in Ohio, Dr. Sam Monroe had demonstrated his expertise and clinical decision-making over the years in his hospitalist role and had been offered the position of medical director of the hospitalists at City Hospital.

Naturally, he excelled in the role and worked diligently to align the functions of the hospitalists with the efficiency of the hospital. He accomplished this primarily with his skills as a seasoned clinician, as a sharp role model for the younger physicians, and with his general affability with the medical staff and administration.

Not unexpectedly, around 2016, Sam was asked to step into a new role at his hospital as a physician advisor. This new, salaried position under the umbrella of Akron City Health, Inc., would report directly to the CMO of the hospital, would partner with the director of case management, and would tackle a variety of new operational challenges for the hospital, including the HRRP and the HAC reporting, and assist in the areas of utilization management (UM) and utilization review (UR).

Sam knew little about these latter two elements and went through a rigorous amount of self-study, seminars, and conferences in his first six months to get up to speed. He continued to take an occasional shift as a hospitalist, mostly on the weekends, but he essentially gave up his 7-on/7-off routine and now worked alongside administrators during the week and assisted case management by mobile phone on the weekends when needed.

His income was roughly equivalent to his hospitalist medical director role — about 15% more than what the hospitalists were earning. But as an added bonus, as a physician advisor, he was offered a chance to earn 10% of his base salary at the end of the fiscal year if the goals set by the CMO and executive leadership were met. Sam was curious enough to take on the new role.

UTILIZATION MANAGEMENT AND UTILIZATION REVIEW

As the payer side of healthcare was undergoing major overhaul with the implementation of CMS in the 1960s, UR was established to reduce overutilization of resources and identify waste. The UR function occurred in hospital settings and out of site of the physicians and was initially performed by registered nurses (RNs) as part of case management and revenue cycle management.

The health insurance industry was keenly invested in these processes, mainly due to growing research about medical necessity, misuse, and overutilization of services.[4] Therefore, health plans also reviewed claims for medical necessity and the hospital length of stay (LOS).

To hold the hospital accountable and contain costs, and to avoid any notion that the health plans were dictating any sort of medical care, some health plans required *a physician* to certify the admission and any subsequent days after the admission.

The idea of physicians certifying the appropriateness of care of a patient they were not treating created a new career for doctors: As one who (aside from a pathologist) might earn a medical degree and be paid to render an opinion without physically caring for a patient.

Briefly, there are three activities within the utilization review process: prospective, concurrent, and retrospective.

Prospective review includes the review of medical necessity for the performance of services or scheduled procedures before admission. *Concurrent review* includes a review of medical necessity decisions made while the patient is currently in an acute or post-acute setting. *Retrospective reviews* involve a review of coverage after treatment is provided.

The overall UR also includes precertification, continued stay review, and transition of care, as well as detailed evaluations of medical necessity, level of care, and delays/progression in care.[4]

If these functions are not carried out with a reasonable degree of exactitude, payers can hold or deny payments, creating significant burdens for the hospitals and the patients (who may be responsible, in some cases, for payment), not to mention for physicians who may not receive professional revenue for their care.

As hospital margins in the past two decades have become increasingly smaller, the responsibilities of case management, UR, and physician advisors have increased with regard to the financial stability of hospital revenue.

MEASURING PATIENT SATISFACTION AND HOSPITAL QUALITY

In 2002, CMS partnered with the Agency for Healthcare Research and Quality (AHRQ) to develop a standardized, publicly reported survey of patients' experiences with their hospital care.[5] The survey, known as the Hospital Consumer Assessment of Healthcare Providers and Systems (HCAHPS), was the first national method

110

of collecting data to measure patient satisfaction with care received at hospitals.

Today, the HCAHPS is comprised of 27 questions, all related to aspects of the patient's hospital experience. CMS rewards and reimburses hospitals based on their performance scores. The quality of care provided to Medicare patients, together with how closely best clinical practices are followed and how well a facility enhances the patient experience of care, are used to determine how much a facility receives in Medicare reimbursement.

By 2017, hospitals were at risk for penalties (or rewards) up to 2% of a hospital's base operating payment.[5] And to make matters even more interesting, CMS began publishing Overall Hospital Quality Star Ratings in 2015 and over time, centered hospitals' base payments on those star ratings.[6]

The ratings include about two-thirds of the more than 100 measures (which are updated periodically) collected by the Hospital Inpatient Quality Reporting (IQR) program and Hospital Outpatient Quality Reporting (OQR) program.[6] Not to be outdone, there are also CMS star ratings programs for Medicare-based health plans, home healthcare, and hospice to name a few.

So, roughly between 2010 and 2020, CMS began to seek measurements of care, track them, and then tie reimbursement to individual programs as well as overall payments (based on star ratings) across the continuum of care of the Medicare beneficiaries.

DIFFERENT DOCTORS, DIFFERENT PERSPECTIVES

Sophie's husband, Dr. Kevin Ramsey, spent a few weeks contemplating his role as medical director and met with the service line director about his responsibilities and his renumeration. Kevin didn't see much promise for his income in the near future and believed that this role might be a path for additional income.

Kevin and the administration had several discussions regarding the money, and during each round, he was faced with concepts about fair market value, timekeeping, Stark Laws, and various others brought forth by the administration.

He ultimately capitulated and took the best offer he could obtain, which was about $200/hour, and with the time commitment, he could foresee an additional $70,000 of annual income.

Kevin figured (rather naively) that he could facilitate the reduction in CHF readmissions, given his status as a prominent cardiologist and with the support from the department members and staff. After a year in the role, there was absolutely no improvement in the readmission rate of CHF and compared to some of the other readmission conditions managed by other service lines (total hip or knee arthroplasty, pneumonia, and COPD) the cardiology service line was not performing well.

On top of that, about four months into the role, the cardiology service line added to Kevin's responsibilities goals around acute myocardial infarction and coronary artery bypass graft readmission reductions.

None of the cardiac-related readmission rates were improving. And at the end of the first year of the contract (albeit originally a two-year agreement), Kevin was given 30 days' notice and the contract was terminated.

During his year in the role, Kevin found that the position took more time and effort than he originally planned, and it cut into his regular patient care activities, not to mention even more work to catch up on at the end of the day.

When he resumed to "full-time" practice (which he never actually ceased), he was relieved to no longer have the administrative burden; however, he found out that he had been losing referrals because of his limited availability at times while attending meetings and working on the readmission goals. It took more than three years to recover his lost volume of patient work and procedures.

Dr. Sam Monroe, on the other hand, rather enjoyed the challenge of the PA role. While he did not particularly care for the UR work, he enjoyed becoming increasingly familiar with the hospital operations.

He raised his awareness of all of the departments, staff, tasks involved in the areas of HRRP, HAC, HCAHPS, and especially the LOS. He missed the daily bedside patient interactions, but he found himself surrounded by clinicians serving in various roles, and all of the efforts felt as though they were improving patient outcomes.

When he first started to tackle the hospital's length of stay, he reviewed months of data and found opportunities to reduce the excess days. Many of the barriers were related to delays in imaging completion, imaging interpretation, procedural scheduling, and discharge placement. There also were delays in consultations, doctor-doctor communications, and weekend discharges held over until Mondays.

Sam focused on the internal barriers and obstacles and saw results almost immediately. Recall that if the payer was going to pay a prospective amount for a given diagnosis, if patients were to stay any longer than the generally accepted LOS, and if theoretically the cost of the care exceeded the revenue, the hospital saw no financial advantage, and possibly a loss of money given that expenses kept accruing.

Even more demonstrative to the hospital finances, if there is an excess in LOS, then there are too many patients occupying the available beds that could otherwise hold a new patient with a new diagnosis and a new DRG payment. And this is lost revenue on top of the ongoing expenses for each day the hospital is not receiving additional payment.

CALCULATING COSTS AND SAVINGS

When Sam had his annual performance review, the CMO congratulated him on the work related to all the stated goals — especially the reduction of the hospital's overall average LOS by 0.2 days (which Sam honestly felt was not much of a reduction).

But what caught Sam by surprise was the CMO said, "Sam, you did a fantastic job. You saved the hospital $3 million. For that, we could have paid you double and still saved the hospital about $2.5 million."

To calculate LOS, let's start with a 500-bed hospital with all types of services, including critical care, various surgeries, labor and delivery, and pediatrics. Knowing that most of the hospital daily expenses occur in the first few days when acuity and needs are high, let's assume an average blended cost of $500/day when a patient occupies an inpatient bed at our hypothetical hospital.

For this exercise, we must recognize that patients with the most serious conditions will cost more while those with lower acuity and shorter stays will cost less. That is why we "blend" the cost into an average.

Now suppose that for the entire hospital, the LOS averages 5.0 and the facility has 30,000 discharges each year. By multiplying 5.0 x 30,000, the hospital experiences 150,000 "patient days." If we use the blended rate at $500/day, those patient days cost the hospital $75 million/year (150,000 × $500).

If the average hospital LOS is reduced to 4.8, the math demonstrates now that the hospital spent $72 million on patient care — a "savings" of $3 million. Each tenth of a day reduction would create $1.5 million in savings.

For the purposes of this exercise, we will not debate whether these are real dollars that are "saved" (as many would argue that it is not the same as buying pharmaceuticals at a discount), but it is still something that accountants track in the hospital financial reports.

When Sam found that he had saved the hospital $3 million he was stunned. Further, when the CMO followed up by saying, "You are worth your weight in gold, you really are," he was really taken aback.

Dr. Kevin Ramsey never really understood what had happened regarding his role and the termination based on his performance. When he tried to learn more about the decision-making, he was told that without an improvement in the readmissions, the finance office could not justify the medical directorship compensation. In fact, he never saw the pro forma that was built around his role. Had he seen it, he may not have understood it, not because of any lack of intelligence or even financial acumen, but rather because of the complexity of the model itself.

To rationalize the directorship, the service line director attempted to map out the financial impact of the readmission penalties against the costs to reduce readmissions, one of which was the cost of Kevin's directorship.

In an exhaustive review of this subject, Yakusheva and Hoffman show how challenging this type of financial modeling is to design.[7] One must consider the baseline number of readmissions, along with the added direct (labor/supplies) and indirect (facility/space) costs required to reduce the readmissions, inherent costs of those index admissions, the renumeration for each condition (e.g., THA/TKA, CHF, AMI), and finally the impact of any penalties.

With those assumptions, one then has to model how much of a reduction might occur (e.g., 5% or 10%), inclusive of how much reimbursement would "vanish" from removing those (re)admissions from the hypothetical future state. One must also take note that the finances are unique to each condition based on acuity, DRG payment, labor, etc., such that each condition requires its own unique modeling.[7]

Anyone who is interested in advancing their CMO role and/or executive career should take the requisite time and read the work of Yakusheva and Hoffman to gain insights into how complex these models look.[7] Regardless, a CMO should develop an understanding of how the money flows when asked to support initiatives that have clinical impact.

Using the HRRP as a case study, consider that the care of a frequently admitted patient with CHF falls under the auspice of quality and patient care, and therefore involves the CMO. The CMO must know how the hospital will support any programming to change the clinical dynamics of such a patient population and should be prepared to think critically about all of the elements required to ensure the proper discharge and care plan.

Again, using CHF readmission reduction as an example, non-clinical administrators are not trained to know about the complexity of CHF and may not understand how critical medication delivery and adherence, daily weights, and access to follow-up, to name a few, are in the management of this illness. Further, these elements all require time and staff to assemble the processes, workflows, and handoffs to reduce the readmission.

To complicate matters, if Kevin's hospital was unknowingly already at a low readmission rate for CHF, then perhaps this was not the right target for everyone. Maybe it distracted from the targeting of AMI or CABG where the resources were better allocated rather than possibly spread too thin among three cardiac conditions.

Finally, what impact would there be on the CMS star ratings if the readmission targets were not met? While the six conditions remain in place for the HRRP, the calculation for CMS star ratings can depend, in part, on how the various VBP programs are measured and inputted.[8] If a particular star rating is a desired goal, how much time and resources does each element in the calculation require?

Not every system is equipped to dive this deep; however, when a star rating can have an overall impact on all CMS based payment to a hospital, it certainly would be beneficial to accomplish due diligence on the matter and to deploy the right amount of time, energy, and costs to achieve the goal.

Remember as well, that all of this activity is overhead that did not exist in the 20th century. So, it follows once more that for the hospital to receive its split of the money, or at least to hold onto its current split, it would have to allocate appropriate overhead to do so.

As the 2000s began, hospitals had to pay increasingly more attention to the shifts in workload required to receive payment for its services, and if those services were not meeting the desired specification of the payer (CMS, in this example), the hospital had to think deeply about its ability to achieve its stated objectives and fulfill its mission.

LESSONS LEARNED

- Payment for service is a bit in the eye of the beholder. Having the payer, rather than the patient, pay for a service influences a great many parts of the care.
- Patients generally pay for an outcome (e.g., an evaluation, a diagnosis, or an intervention), but payers began to pay for process improvements, mostly to reduce their own expenditures. Even if supportive of a better clinical outcome, they were paying hospitals for better processes. But CMS does not pay (i.e., incentivize) the physicians for any new decisions or clinical skills in the provided care.
- The influence of payers on the delivery of care has created a great deal of activity and presumably a new layer of cost for the service providers.

- Penalties were a new way of directing the flow of money in healthcare. Unlike capitation when all of the money is paid up front for providers to use accordingly, CMS penalties to facilities created new risk assessment and demanded new decision-making skills.
- Whether through salary or timesheets, physician compensation for time, rather than services rendered, becomes a new instrument. Is time something that can be split up?

QUESTIONS TO ASK

- Do you know your value as a medical director, physician advisor, VPMA, or CMO?
- Should you advocate for having a value assigned to those roles?
- Do you produce value? Are you simply overhead? Do you know how to identify value? What resources should you have to produce value?
- Who reports to you? What departments are under your authority? If you don't have those resources, are you in a position to articulate the value of having them?
- Do you have access to members of the finance team and/or the data itself to ascertain your patient days, number of discharges, average cost of a day in a hospital bed?
- Have you access to the direct financial impacts of the HCAHPs, or any of the various Consumer Assessment of Healthcare Providers and Systems, upon your department or division, and/or impact on CMS star ratings and related overall payments?
- Should physician leaders be paid for their time? Should they be paid based on outcomes? Or both?
- Do financial goals increase the workload of physicians? If so, how much? What workflows or processes can be constructed to keep the physician working at the top of their skill set? Can you obtain resources to lessen workloads on physicians? What is the value of lowering workload?

- What happens when initiative goals are met and you no longer "bring" new value into the system? Are you rewarded for simply keeping the *status quo*? How do you seek new opportunities to bring value into your system?
- Can a CMO exert influence on the alignment of system goals with local controls and create value for the staff as well as the organization?

Chapter 11

Value-Based Care

"What's in a name? That which we call a rose
by any other name would smell as sweet."

William Shakespeare,

"Romeo and Juliet"

Dr. Sam Monroe became intrigued by hospital operations and equally more interested in learning about the significant role utilization review/utilization management (UR/UM) played in the flow of money to and from the insurers.

He continued to study and learn about how case management oversees areas such as bed status (outpatient in a bed, inpatient), the accurate way of defining an observation status, and the two-midnight rule, all of which are intimately tied to the payment made to the hospital.

Taking a simplistic view, UR/UM is an entire ecosystem devoted to adequately characterizing the type of care that a patient receives to match the right payment for the right services. The hospital's revenue cycle team depends heavily on the UR/UM processes to receive the appropriate payment allowed for the right level of care of the patient.

As Sam became more sophisticated with his utilization acumen, he became aware of another piece of the revenue ecosystem devoted entirely to something known as clinical documentation.

In addition to the level of care, payments are tied to the DRG classification system, but the assignment of the DRG is complex. Under the rules established by CMS, the codes used to assign the appropriate diagnosis are extensive and somewhat restrictive in that the bulk of the assignment is drawn directly from the note entered into the chart by the physician or another provider. Upon discharge, the notes in the chart are finalized and any attempt to amend the document for coding purposes is essentially prohibited.

In reviewing the patient's medical record, coding specialists look for information to support the most appropriate coding to submit the most accurate claim. Most providers are unaware, for example, that while they may assess a patient as having CHF, there isn't one single DRG for CHF; that each DRG in the CHF group can be characterized as with or without a major complication; and that each of those characterizations ought to be connected to a principal diagnosis and a detailed description (e.g., acute vs. chronic, systolic vs. diastolic, right chamber vs. left, etc.) in the chart. This creates a "weight" for the DRG and payment is determined by the level of detail and weight. As one would expect, the more weight, the higher the payment.

Sam's hospital, realizing the vast sums of money involved, developed a clinical documentation improvement (CDI) program under its revenue cycle team to capture the most accurate picture of the patient's condition for the purposes of billing.

When claims are submitted to CMS, a case mix index (CMI) is established based on the sum of all of the DRG weights divided by the number of discharges. Further, the CMI is tied to the payment rate to the hospital. Those hospitals with a higher CMI see a bump in the rate of payment made.

Sam knew from his experience as a hospitalist that he would often be asked to clarify something in the medical record (often known as a "query"), but until undertaking his PA role, he did not quite understand what was happening in the background. In response to an alert from the CDI team, the physician could clarify the chart note, leading to a better DRG classification (i.e., weight) and higher payment to the hospital.

As a physician, Sam never saw any personal compensation for that adjustment. As a PA, he realized he could work collaboratively with the hospitalists and the CDI team to potentially improve the chart documentation more than the team could do alone. He believed this would continue to demonstrate his value to the hospital.

EVER-EVOLVING CMS PAYMENT MODELS

Meanwhile, Sophie was also moving up on her learning curve in the clinic world that she inhabited at JMED. Her ability to manage the EHR had not improved much, and she, along with others, were advocating for a new EHR system.

As a result of her advocacy, she had been volunteered to serve on a committee that would investigate a new EHR that claimed to have the right build to take advantage of a variety of new alternative payment models (APMs) recently announced by CMS.

The EHR company also believed its software was prepared for upcoming changes by private commercial health insurance companies that would shift toward alternative "value purchasing" payment models as well.

Sustainable Growth Rate Algorithm

Sophie's committee was to render a recommendation to JMED's board of directors about the EHR ease of use and to validate the company's claims regarding billing and payments under future models.

She and her fellow committee members felt reasonably assured that they could address ease of use fairly well; however, to understand future payments, they had to quickly educate themselves on the current state.

Recall that in the late 1980s, CMS had established the RBRV scale to determine what healthcare professional fees ought to be "worth" and, from there, the elements of the RVU and the conversion factor that would assign a dollar amount to the base unit.

In the late 1990s, Congress, under pressure to control CMS spending, legislated the sustainable growth rate (SGR) algorithm intended to set a growth rate target for Medicare expenditures based on changes in enrollment, overall economic growth, and a measure of provider efficiency.

In theory, this captured what had been missed in the 1960s when Medicare began. As the population aged and enrolled in Medicare, as the economy changed pricing of goods and services, and as providers carried out more care, naturally Medicare would spend more money each year to cover its beneficiaries. The SGR formula was an attempt to predict whether actual spending would or would not exceed the SGR target and the formula would adjust the conversion factor up or down accordingly.

The expanding economy of the late 1990s elevated the SGR targets and the SGR actually afforded moderate increases in physician payments. But when the economy turned in 2001 and the country experienced the first recession since the formulas were created, the SGR targets demanded that Medicare spending growth slow down as well.

Thus, the formula worked in the opposite direction and cut the monetary conversion factor by up to 4.4%, delivering a pay cut to physicians carrying out the same functions as the prior year.[1]

Needless to say, this was wildly unpopular, and after 2001, Congress continually replaced SGR cuts with moderate payment increases. This naturally pumped more money out of CMS than was originally designed and actual expenditures continuously exceeded each annual SGR target which, as a result of the algorithm, forced further downward adjustments in the conversion factor.

Congress felt even more pressure to avoid cutting physician payments and placed a cap on the size of the cut to the conversion factor, limiting cuts of between 3% and 5%.[1]

For the next decade and a half, the physician payment formula saw virtually no increases, essentially paying the same dollar amount —or in some years, less — for the same office visit year after year.[1]

The Medicare Access and CHIP Reauthorization Act

After a series of legislative tricks to manage the conundrum that was created, the situation reached an untenable level of fiscal responsibility, and a new solution was proposed. On April 16, 2015, President Obama signed into law the Medicare Access and CHIP Reauthorization Act of 2015 (MACRA), which permanently repealed the SGR payment formula for physician reimbursement under Medicare.[1]

This sweeping change required CMS to implement, by 2019, a new two-track payment system for physicians. One of these tracks, the new merit-based incentive payment system (MIPS) tied any increase in physician payments to outcomes. The other track included a variety of APMs that moved payment away from fee-for-service reimbursement altogether and was based on the quality and cost of care for particular episodes or defined patient populations.

While Dr. Sophie Liontari was getting caught up on the new acronyms and implications, her old pal Dr. Sam Monroe was bringing more value to himself in relation to the hospital. His involvement in the CDI program increased the hospital's CMI and this resulted in an increased payment rate to the hospital and more net revenue.

Although none of the newfound skills that Sam acquired were learned in medical school or had anything to do with the delivery of care, his training and experience paid off since his knowledge of diseases and interventions could be applied to the revenue enhancement of the hospital.

As for the hospitalists he worked with on the CDI program, they walked a tightrope between delivering high-quality care and trying to be accurate in the documentation without spending too much time documenting in the chart.

Sam began to hear some rumbles that the physicians were increasingly unhappy with the time spent in the medical record at the expense of interacting with the patients or other clinicians to improve the care of the patient.

While the hospital was pleased with Sam as the physician advisor, Sam was not so sure he was pleased with himself once he had mastered the new skills and created some distress for his fellow physicians. With his efforts to improve LOS and CDI, he wasn't sure if he was making anyone's life any better, and certainly could not directly display any improvements in clinical outcomes.

Sophie and the JMED EHR committee evaluated the new payment models along with the role of a new EHR. The first thing they realized is that to be paid under the MIPs track or the APM track, they would have to re-engineer some workflows and reporting. They quickly concluded that MIPS was combining two prior elements of

MU (*quality measure reporting* and the *resource use* of a certified EHR) with clinical practice improvement activities, and that as the practice was currently constructed, unless the current EHR could adapt to the new reporting, the practice might lose an opportunity to enhance the payments to the practice.

This felt like "déjà vu all over again" as Yogi Berra once said, as the committee would have to recommend to the board that a financial analysis be conducted to determine if any new EHR investment would benefit the practice.

Because MIPS and APMs are constantly changing, it's best for readers to review the information on CMS.gov. As examples of MIPS, suffice it to say that a practice might report the percentage of patients with elevated hemoglobin A1c levels, or the percentage of patients receiving antiplatelet therapy for cardiovascular disease.[2] As for APMs, examples include enhanced payments for providing care navigation or for discussion/documentation of a qualified care plan.[2]

Again, whether there were increased payment rates for all claims or lump payments based on episodic care, the intent was to replace SGR adjustments with these new payments by paying for new programs, services, care delivery, or quality reporting, thus keeping physician payments static. And, once more, this required practitioner investment into the design and implementation of such things.

We can also see once more that CMS was rearranging its payment methods from the pure fees for service of the 1970s–1980s to the modern era of payment for models of care as another way of splitting the money flowing from payer to physician. Perhaps it would have been easier to add a fourth component to the wRVU and to call it "model effort" or "quality effort," but, alas, that did not occur.

RAF and ACO

In parallel to MIPS and APMs, CMS also designed and implemented a wide range of other reimbursement opportunities for physicians and other participants in care. The two most notable and widely adopted include the use of risk adjustment factors (RAF) and accountable care organizations (ACOs).

Recall from Chapter 9 that Medicare beneficiaries were able to participate in HMO-like programs (Medicare + Choice) to reduce their own out-of-pocket expenses. Today, these are more widely recognized as Medicare Advantage (MA) programs managed by commercial insurers.

Under these programs, CMS once more established methods for linking the complexity of the patient care and/or the population served by an MA plan to the payment for the patients.

Like Sam's efforts with CDI in assigning the most detailed documentation to the most appropriate code for hospital payment purposes, practices could render RAF scores on patients covered by an MA plan, which in turn supported potentially increased payments from CMS to the plan and its providers.

Structured in the ambulatory environment, RAF scoring is yet another way of describing the acuity of a patient such that payment is aligned with the level of "work" involved to care for such a person. But, unlike in the hospital, physicians in practice may see a share of this assigned payment depending on its arrangements with the insurance company that is managing the MA patient plans. As such, care delivery and professional services were diverging in both payments and care models.

Physicians who worked in both offices and hospitals might see differences in how they were paid depending on the environment of care; even if they did not see it in the payment, they certainly would have felt it in the work expended to receive the renumeration. In some cases, work in the office took on a variety of new tasks in order to be paid at the going rate, or work in the hospital was more complex and/or time consuming, but without direct compensation.

Finally, CMS attempted to influence bridging these gaps with attention to the continuum of care by virtue of the accountable care organization (ACO).

The model of an ACO is linked to the more recent changing dynamic wherein physicians are paid to manage the health of populations rather than based on the volume of services they provide. We saw this in Chapter 3 during the booming era of commercial managed care and HMOs in the 1980s and the various forms of "network" designs.

Between 2005 and 2010, CMS began its efforts with the Pioneer ACO pilot program to foster ACOs, any of which would include a group of healthcare providers (physicians, hospitals, non-physician providers, etc.) coming together and collectively agreeing to become responsible for the financial and quality outcomes for a defined population.[3]

By 2012, CMS was well on its way to providing the accompanying payment models that shifted financial risk from CMS to the group of providers in an ACO, particularly under the newly created Medicare Shared Savings Program.[3]

Similar to MIPs and APMs, the ACO groups had to measure and report on a variety of process improvements along with appropriate risk stratification of the beneficiaries to be paid appropriately.

Some of those payments were made as "per member per month," similar to capitation, and in some cases additional payments were not distributed until the performance measures were submitted and audited; either way, providers were strongly incentivized to change how they were delivering care with the goals of decreasing spending while improving quality measures and patient satisfaction.

If you recall from Chapter 7, it has the feel of capitation, in part by paying upfront for services rendered and by shifting the risk to the provider side. However, in the ACO iteration, the money was at least partly tied to quality and performance.

This is also an area in which the notion of "shared savings" entered the vernacular, as it became another potential incentive for profitability through care management by the providers.

PHYSICIAN PRACTICE MANAGEMENT REDUX

With the initiation of MIPS/APMs/ACOs, the physician practice management companies (see Chapter 6) resurfaced under different structures as well. One such company, Privia Health, was founded in 2007, and labeled itself as a "physician enablement company" with a "focus on reducing physicians' administrative burdens, accelerating the transition to value-based care and helping physicians adopt user-friendly technology to better engage patients."[4]

The company enabled the physicians with the tools, education, analytics, and workflow to help them move to value-based care over time through the use of technology, its proprietary EHR, and its scale to achieve large ACO structures.[5]

Some of the more recent Privia performance highlights include a lower ED utilization, lower outpatient and inpatient facility utilization, higher PCP utilization, and an overall decrease in expenditures compared to other MSSP participating ACOs or compared to fee-for-service Medicare (for a similar population).[5]

Further, Privia also maintains a large enough number of physician portfolios under its structure that it can competitively negotiate commercial contracts for its physicians and those same physician practices are NOT owned by Privia — a twist from the PPM days.

In return for all of these services, it has been reported that Privia charges the practice a fee of 12% on any fee-for-service payment and 40% on any value-based service payment.[6]

Had Sophie known about companies such as Privia, she might have encouraged the committee to recommend that the board consider joining an ACO in partnership with such a company that could deliver a new EHR and software to capture the required measurements for the APMs, along with leverage to secure higher commercial insurance payment rates. This would accomplish the goal of delivering a solvent and sustainable way to upgrade the EHR and netting an increase in revenue without requiring a new capital partnership or a sale of the practice.

PHYSICIANS' CHOICE

Sam and Sophie were colleagues during her education in Akron, albeit Sam was a few years ahead of Sophie in the trajectory of medical education. They both, however, had strong skills in internal medicine, regardless of whether they provided care inside a hospital or in an office. In the span of only about a decade, Sam's and

Sophie's careers had drifted about as far apart from each other's in ways that they had never imagined back in residency.

Nothing in their education or training prepared them for the rapid changes in structure, payment, or work effort required to care for patients as independent professionals. Neither of them could even begin to gather all of the moving parts quickly enough to see the big picture, much less the landscape from a suborbital view. They were doing the best they could under the circumstances while remaining attentive to their immediate roles and responsibilities.

But while they were hundreds of miles apart and separated by different architectures of care, they individually and independent of each other decided to make radical decisions that would stay with them for the rest of their careers.

LESSONS LEARNED

- Time spent away from direct patient care is not reimbursable in the traditional fee-for-service payer equations unless it is incorporated into the "work" component of the wRVU. Neither practice expense or malpractice would change, nor would the work payment increase, but new payment designs were attempting to compensate the added work incurred with complex patient populations.
- Time spent documenting medical conditions is precious time, but the value of that time depends on who is spending it and who is compensated for it. The value may also depend on what else could be done with the same units of time (e.g., direct patient care, reading medical literature, family time, etc.).
- CMOs need to be knowledgeable about the various CMS payment models and develop a strategy to keep up to date. While they do not necessarily need to be subject matter experts on any one model, they need to be alert to changes/ modifications. It would behoove any CMO to have regular engagement with team leaders involved in finance, coding, managed care, revenue cycle, etc.

- Currently evolving payment models are requiring shifts in physician workload and care delivery, none of which are learned while in medical school or residency when physicians are attempting to master a set of professional skills to diagnose and treat those with health issues.
- CMOs must be prepared to lead efforts around adaptability and to be able to weigh in on the role of cost, infrastructure, training, and performance to adopt new models successfully.
- The landscape of care delivery continues to widen between care of the sickest and most critically ill within hospitals and the chronically ill and reasonably active in the ambulatory settings and those who are chronically institutionalized, such as the elderly or severely disabled. While not discussed in this chapter, there is also widening of the care of those who have reasonable access to care and those who do not.
- The divergence of care and the payment models behind them continued the trend of tension between those who provide the care ("who is on call") and how to "split up the money." Furthermore, some physicians care for highly specialized elements of a patient's condition under static fees, while others care for populations under capitated like arrangements.

QUESTIONS TO ASK

- Is it appropriate that physicians must be masters of clinical documentation in order to be professionals?
- What is the role of a CMO when the organization seeks to leverage his or her skills as a physician to translate the clinical mastery into revenue?
- Is it appropriate that payers pay more for more complex care? Alternatively, should physicians be incentivized to reduce complexity of care? Who benefits under each structure?
- If physicians are to be incentivized to reduce complexity, shouldn't the physicians be adequately rewarded? How

should the physician and the payer share in the reduction of long-term costs? Is this what is meant by "shared savings"?

- What exactly are payers "purchasing" in value-based care? Is it process-based care? Is value-based care, just fee-for-service by another name, and payers are asking for different services?
- Is accountable care another form of capitation, in part or in whole, but with a different service that the providers are now accountable for?
- Who has control within value-based payment models?
- When did physicians lose control of their ability to set pricing for their skills? If the payers were seeking different skills, who should have been delivering those skills?
- What were patients seeking in these various models? Quality outcomes? Quality experiences?

CHAPTER 12

Physician Compensation

"If you don't know where you are going,
you'll end up someplace else."

Yogi Berra

". . . remember, no matter where you go, there you are."

Buckaroo Banzai

NOT LONG AFTER Dr. Sam Monroe had established himself as a valuable physician advisor, the CMO of City Hospital was elevated to a more senior position within the Akron City Health system, and Sam was encouraged to apply for the soon-to-be-vacant CMO position.

Sam was interviewed along with a few other outstanding candidates from outside the system, and after a couple of rounds of internal deliberations, the CEO decided none of the other candidates had demonstrated as much value to their respective organizations as had Sam.

When Sam received a phone call that the role was his should he choose to accept, he took the weekend to think it over and called the CEO first thing on Monday to ask when he could start. The CEO told Sam to provide him with his PA succession plan and to be ready to start in two weeks.

Shortly after beginning the new role, Sam was scheduled into a meeting with the hospital's COO, CFO, and CEO. The only individual missing from the hospital executive team was the CNO. The topic of the meeting was "physician contracts."

Sam had no preparation for the meeting and felt that with only a few days under his belt as CMO, there would not be a lot of expectations regarding his participation. He could not have been more wrong.

The meeting was relatively brief, with a lot of varied opinions expressed in very short order. It ended with Sam being given the responsibility not only to manage all hospital-based physicians, but to lead the negotiations for the renewal of the contracts of the hospitalist and the emergency department physicians.

He had a lot of experience as a hospitalist, as a prior medical director, and as a physician advisor, not to mention that he learned a lot about physician compensation when AMG acquired his group many years ago. However, he knew much less about the ED physicians.

The executive team gave him two mandates: lower by $2 million the expense of having these two groups under contract and engage the ED physicians on a variety of ED physician-related throughput measures to improve the overall ED metrics. Some of these included triage time, percentage of "left without being seen," and door to discharge.

The COO was under pressure to improve overall hospital throughput, some of which was bogged down in the ED, starting with ED wait times. The CFO was under pressure to lower expenses by several million dollars and had determined with the prior CMO that the hospital-based physician contracts were "too rich." And the CEO was under pressure from the system C-suite to be more "presidential" and run a tighter ship.

Sam had no idea that any of this had been underway when he was offered the CMO role, nor did he have any expectation that he would be called upon so quickly to manage such major issues. Nonetheless, he buckled down and got to work.

He immediately asked for copies of the hospitalist and ED physician contracts and asked to see financial reports of both programs. He scheduled meetings right away with the administrative directors of the two groups and in advance of the meetings sent each a series of questions that he wished to be addressed when they gathered.

He also made sure that he would have time on his schedule to meet with the hospitalist medical director and the CEO of the ED physician group, a physician who, like Sam many years prior, had created an independent group of physicians to provide their services to City Hospital.

Sam was taking an inventory of the current situation and would create a mental situation report to be filed away for later use. After he had his ducks in a row, he asked the CEO for permission to place "physician contracting" on the next executive team agenda so that he could provide an update of his work.

During the executive team meeting, he stunned the team by asking permission to seek a request for proposal (RFP) from other hospital-based physician organizations, particularly those that have a national footprint. He also asked that, if granted permission to conduct the RFP, the team would keep this confidential and that any meetings or face-to-face proposal reviews would take place away from the hospital.

When the executive team asked why he wanted to do this, his answer was that there was no way to accomplish the two mandates without separating from the current contracted groups. They were surprised at the speed of his findings and his resultant suggestion, and they acquiesced quickly to his request.

AMG, the employer of the hospitalists at City Hospital, provided each hospitalist with a standard physician employment agreement (PEA). Under each PEA, the physicians were now earning a base salary of $280,000 and potentially more if they exceeded the base expected "productivity." It appeared now that at a salary of $280,000 with a productivity of 4,000 wRVUs, the physicians were being paid at a rate of $70/wRVU.

BASIC FINANCES OF PHYSICIAN COMPENSATION

When Sam's group agreed to be acquired, the physicians were paid $62/wRVU and at 4,000 wRVUs, Sam earned about $250,000. How did the $/RVU go up so much while he was a physician advisor and away from the employed hospitalist role?

To understand the market conditions of physician employment contracting, we must dive a little deeper into some basic finances of physician compensation.

When Sam was in private practice, his group managed all of the billings and all of the overhead of running the practice. When he visited a patient in the hospital and performed a follow-up visit, he billed for the service and his office submitted the claim. Once the money was collected and expenses paid, he took home what was left.

For such a visit, Medicare might pay $93.80, but Blue Cross might pay 125% of Medicare at $117.25. If Sam generated two-thirds of his payments from Medicare and one-third from Blue Cross, he might generate a blended payment of roughly $100.60 for his follow-up hospital visits, assuming all of the claims were paid at 100%. Sam was entitled to "keep" the entire payment, as he managed his practice expense and the malpractice expense of his professional service.

When the practice was acquired, however, Sam's group achieved only about 85% in collections for all of the billings. Part of the reason it is not 100% (and it hardly ever is), is that patients who are responsible for a co-pay or who are self-pay do not always pay their billed share, not to mention denials from insurance carriers. So, the practice received a blended net collection of about $85 for each of this type of hospital follow-up visit.

Under an RVU system, let's say a follow-up hospital visit (coded as CPT 99222) is converted into 2.68 RVUs (1 RVU for practice expense, 0.38 RVU for malpractice, and 1.3 for the work RVU) and the conversion factor is $35. Because the employed physician is no longer responsible for the practice expense or malpractice expense, even if the hospital received 100% of a typical Medicare payment, Sam is not entitled to the gross $93.80 (2.68 × $35) from Medicare, as the hospital has to manage all of the physician's expenses of practice.

Again, if the current hospitalists were being compensated at $70/wRVU, it would also seem at first glance that the hospital is still keeping $23.80 on each of these visits ($93.80 – $70).

When Sam collected his 85% in private practice, he had to pay for all of the overhead of the practice expenses which, at the time of the practice sale, was about 50%. As such, he only took home $42.50 for "work" of his hospital visit ($100 blended rate × 85% collection × 50% overhead).

At first glance, once more, it appears that the hospital offers a better structure for compensating employed physicians. But that is not quite the case.

When the hospital employs a physician to provide the same follow-up visit or service to the patient, the hospital also has overhead expenses, often referred to as corporate expense, overhead expense, overhead allocation, corporate allocation, or shared allocation.

In our example, let's also say that the hospital's collection for a single professional service (hospital follow-up visit) of a Medicare patient is almost always going to be 100% ($93.80 = 2.68 RVU × $35 CF) but the overhead expense might be close to 75%, so the net patient revenue would be $65.55 ($93.80 × .75).

So, the hospital is not generating a positive margin when paying the hospitalists; in fact, they are actually losing $4.34 ($70 − $65.66) on Medicare patients! And, if the overall hospital collections for physician services across all payers are no better than the private practice at 85%, the net patient revenue for all billings (using the same hypothetical blended rate as above) would amount to $63.75 (100 × .85 × .75), which is even worse!

Now that he was the CMO, Sam could see the system finances, specifically the payer mix, blended rates, collections, and expenses, from the "other side" and realized that the hospital was actually subsidizing the physician compensation since the hospital was creating a negative margin.

Why must an employer subsidize so much of the physician income? It harkens back to "usual and customary." Years ago, when physicians determined their fees and CMS tried to create formulas (RBRVs) to account for the fees it would pay, and then created yet more formulas to limit overall expenditures (SGR, RVUs,) in the face of growing services, higher utilization, more beneficiaries, longer life span, etc., physicians continued to work hard to maintain their base incomes. It was those incomes that set the market standard for salaried compensation, which goes to basic economic principles of supply and demand.

The City Hospital system was strategically positioning itself in its market and needed employed hospitalists to achieve its goals of efficient hospital operations and to manage competition for care and services. There was a demand for physicians and the supply dictated the price.

If ACH were to employ the hospitalist group, it would have to pay handsomely. When Sam's partners did the math and determined that they probably could not work much harder and that they did not see any opportunities for ancillary services, capital partners, physician enablement companies, the hospital and the health system appeared to be the only logical partner to maintain their incomes.

So, when AMG offered to acquire the practice, despite any feelings of paranoia or concern by the physicians, the "splitting of the money" naturally drove the group to sell to AMG and move to the new contracted employment.

Surprisingly (at least to him), Sam's initial review of the current hospitalist finances showed that the system did not collect enough money from those 4,000 wRVUs to cover the $280,000 base salary. Years ago, Sam was uninterested in these equations, but he was also unable to learn more facts when negotiating his practice buyout and new employment contracts. Now that he was the CMO, he could see the system finances, specifically the payer mix, blended rates, and collections from the "other side," and he found that the hospital had only been able to collect about $60/wRVU, also known as net patient revenue per wRVU.

The administrative expenses of a hospital were sizably larger than those of a practice, especially when the hospitals were part of a larger system. Remember, too, that as employees, physicians enjoyed benefits such as health insurance, 401k plans, paid time off, and CME stipends that are structured quite differently in a small office and must be accounted for by the employer.

With all of those benefits (which can amount to about 25% of someone's income), on average, the hospital was subsidizing (or "supporting") the physician salary by about $110,000, which was well below what other systems were known to be spending.

Today, the average subsidy per physician/FTE is anywhere from $200,000 to $280,000 and varies by geography, employer model, system structure, and site of care (ambulatory vs. inpatient). Be mindful of the size of this number in your organization.

In the early 2000s, as more physicians became employed under contract, market forces dictated rising physician compensation as a result of supply and demand. While those salaries have largely been flat of late, there was certainly a new normal by the time Sam became CMO. Employers were increasingly relying on practice benchmarks across a region to determine comparable salaries across similar settings.

At the time of the contract renewal under Sam's authority as CMO, hospitalists were being paid about $280,000, and at 4,000 wRVU, the rate was "backed into" and thus amounted to $70/wRVU. Which came first, the salary or the rate, has long been forgotten. So, even with the new understanding of the finances, Sam was left with the market conditions that would dictate the "going rate."

What was not clear to Sam was whether or not the hospital could cut the rate and achieve any type of savings as mandated without the physicians choosing to not renew and walk out the door. Hence, Sam decided to source other hospitalist groups in case this happened.

LESSONS LEARNED

- The more the money was split up and diverging in different directions, the larger systems grew in order to keep the whole pie to themselves.
- This pie growth also added increasing amount of administrative work and expense, so it kept fostering more integration of models.
- Employed physicians are seen as a direct cost to a system. Any revenue that is generated by physician work is captured in facility fees, ancillary services, etc. Just as practices sought to enhance ancillary services to generate revenue, large systems use physician labor to do the same thing.
- Physicians generate large amounts of dollars through cognitive and procedural services, and also spin off the "technical/facility" dollars to the system. Most systems, therefore,

account for employed physicians as "the cost of doing business."

- Hospitalists are unique in that they have only one source of revenue and that is professional revenue for the care of patients. The work is cognitive and requires documentation. The compensation for hospitalists is more simplified.
- Other medical specialists, such as cardiologists, have additional sources of professional revenue such as when the work is procedural (documentation required, too) or interpretative (e.g., electrocardiogram, echocardiogram, catheter film, nuclear imaging). Those services have CPT codes and corresponding wRVUs (also subjected to payer mix, collection, overhead, etc.) but the net patient revenue applies just as well.
- For surgeons/surgical specialists, their professional revenue for surgery and follow-up care may fall under global payment models (lump sum prepayments) and which may create subtle complexities for determining net patient revenue, but the general principle still applies.
- The point is for the CMO to know how physicians manage billing and collections in private practice compared to how the model is converted and how it works under employment.

QUESTIONS TO ASK

- As one follows the flow of money, do you perceive employed physicians as a cost to the system? Is it because professional services alone do not cover the salary? Should physicians be able to "cover" their salary? Is this a hospital/health system issue or a systemic issue regarding reimbursement?
- Are health systems to be considered the newest version of a capital partner for physicians? Or a holding company of sorts? The company (i.e., hospital/health system) holds access to capital and dispenses dollars to the physicians based on their work.
- How do CFOs account for the upstream or downstream revenue to the hospital, group, or health system provided

by employing physicians? How do they value physicians? Or are employed physicians simply seen as the cost of doing business?

CHAPTER 13

Physician Contracting/ Contracted Staffing

Jim Garrison: "I never realized Kennedy was so dangerous to the establishment. Is that why?"

X: "Well that's the real question, isn't it? Why?... Why was Kennedy killed? Who benefited? Who has the power to cover it up? Who?"

Oliver Stone, "JFK"

DR. SAM MONROE MET WITH REPRESENTATIVES of four physician contracting groups. Two of them offered both ED and hospitalist services, one offered only hospitalist services, and one offered only ED services.

Sam reviewed all four proposals in depth. There was a definite common thread for the hospitalist models. All of the physician staffing companies offered their ability to improve the hospital metrics, particularly the LOS and CDI, both of which Sam had conquered when he was the physician advisor.

There was a subtle difference, however, in that Sam had attacked the problem for the entire hospital and had worked every department of the medical staff. Sam proved that lowering the LOS for the entire hospital, even by a small increment, provided tremendous savings.

He did not, however, have the bandwidth to focus just on the employed hospitalist and to drill down on each and every member of the team. Likewise, he did not have the ability to drill down on each independent physician. He had boiled the ocean, as they say, rather than the pot of water right in front of him.

TAKING STAFFING OUTSIDE

The outside agencies showed Sam data plots and graphs of their teams at similarly sized hospitals where they were under contract and showed him how they accounted for each and every physician.

Starting with a DRG such as simple congestive heart failure, they could display a physician's number of cases in a 90-day period along with that individual physician's average LOS and CDI/CMI for those patient cases. This would generate a total charge (based on payer) and actual payment.

They showed Sam how they worked with that client hospital to understand its fixed and variable costs and to determine a net patient revenue per physician. All of their staff physicians provided a contribution (margin) to the hospital.

They could even display individual all-cause 30-day readmissions, CHF readmissions, and HCAHPs scores, all of which were at or near the benchmarks for top performance.

The companies also shared that with those excellent metrics they had been able to negotiate premium payments from commercial insurance companies, which allowed them to pay the physicians a handsome salary.

Finally, they offered to hire (or not) any of the physicians currently under contract with Sam and would work carefully with legal counsel in the event that Sam's doctors had non-compete clauses in their PEAs (which, of course, they did).

At first blush, Sam felt as though the staffing companies offered a product that would benefit the hospital. He was initially enthusiastic about the potential benefits to the hospital; however, when he began to consider the request from his CFO to trim millions of dollars from the expense of paying hospitalists, Sam had to pivot and ask the crucial questions of the staffing companies: How much would the staffing cost the hospital? What did the contract cost? What would the ROI look like? Would there be a net savings?

Sam received similar answers from each company, which was to say that for a reasonable price, the staffing companies could offer their services which would be of value to the hospital.

In other words, if the hospital agreed to the price tag, the staffing company could assure the hospital that it would pay no more than it was currently paying for its hospitalists, because the staffing firm would improve LOS and CDI/CMI to offset and reduce excess days and improve revenue to offset the added expense.

Further, the staffing companies had contracts in place with commercial insurers that paid for professional services at a premium compared to the current hospital payments. The staffing companies would manage all of the physician billing and collecting, which would also reduce the manpower of the hospital for those same functions.

The math looked favorable to the hospital. The facility could reduce the expenses of its revenue team devoted to hospitalist billing, it could see a lift in the CMI by virtue of improved documentation (CDI), and benefit from a further reduction in LOS for patients under the care of the hospitalists under the staffing contract — not to mention better patient satisfaction scores and reduced readmissions along with improvements in other CMS value-based measures of quality care.

A LOOK BEHIND THE SCENES

Sam considered all of the data but felt uneasy. He could not quite understand how the staffing companies could achieve these goals while, under the current arrangement, the hospital could not do so by itself. What did the hospitalist staffing companies offer that the hospital did not?

So, Sam did what any reasonable fellow would do: He called one of his colleagues from his residency days who happened to work for one of the agencies and asked what was happening behind the scenes. His colleague, Geoff, was more than willing to share his insights, so long as Sam promised full confidentiality.

Geoff shared first that the PEAs for the employed physicians in the staffing company offered shares of the company as part of the compensation. Second, the staffing company routinely engaged in contracts with insurance companies that did NOT have contracts with the hospitals. In those arrangements, the staffing company could bill the insurance companies as "out of network" and send the patients bills for services that were "out of network."

These bills were often the source of additional revenue that the hospital was unable to obtain under its prior hospitalist model and corresponding contracts in place. This was a key source of additional revenue that Sam could not receive under the current arrangements.

Geoff also shared that his company was owned, in part, by outside investors, and that those investors expected a significant return on their investment. It was not a physician-run company, but rather a business enterprise that sought to benefit from taking a larger slice of the revenue pie through higher bills.

Geoff implied that the staffing companies used the narrative of efficient LOS and improved CDI to entice hospitals to contract with the companies as a "win-win" for both parties. But in reality, hospitals paid the staffing company enough money to effectively subsidize the contracted physician salaries, and with the added revenue from both premium contracts and out-of-network collections, the company had a healthy operating income (i.e., margin) and the doctors had "skin in the game" with some of their compensation paid in deferred stock shares.

Similarly, the contracted ED physician models worked in much the same way, but those physicians had no direct impact on LOS or CDI. The ED physicians, however, could foster improvements in throughput and efficiency by tightly managing the flow of patients in and out of the ED with reduced wait times, careful assessment of observation care vs. inpatient admission, reductions in "left without being seen," and similar metrics.

A substantial portion of the throughput of any medium or large sized hospital depends on the workflows in their emergency departments and the ease of admission into the hospital, not to mention the value of "treat and release" patients.

And, as far as the hospital was concerned, the facility payments that were produced by a high-volume ED were critical from a cash flow perspective. A constipated ED leads to a lack of revenue, and a bloated, sluggish hospital can do the same thing to the ED by reducing the ability of patients to be placed in beds upstairs.

Sam asked Geoff if he knew anything about the ED side of the physician contracting and Geoff replied with additional information unknown to Sam at the time.

When the staffing company moved into his hospital's environment, they hired advanced practice practitioners (APPs) such as nurse practitioners and physician assistants and reduced the number of physicians on the payroll in both the hospitalist arrangement and in the ED. This lowered the salary costs of the company but maintained the same level of productivity regarding patient throughput.

The company also paid modest stipends to a moderate number of hospitalists and ED doctors to serve as team leaders/medical directors "to keep the trains running on time." These individuals spent time in an internal company leadership program that equipped them with new skills (along with new expectations) to keep things moving in the desired direction of the company.

While those goals were not necessarily in conflict with the hospital goals, they were not necessarily in alignment either.

In both scenarios, the staffing companies asked the hospital for a percentage of the physician salary to be paid by the hospital, as well as a "management" fee.

Remember (Chapter 6) how physicians in private practice sought better billing/collection systems to achieve higher net revenue by partnering with managed service companies? Does this seem familiar to you now? The physician staffing agency representatives told Sam that they could bill and collect for their doctors at a fraction of what it would cost the hospital, and even with the agency fee, it would be lower than the hospital's current internal costs for the same function.

MAPPING THE FLOW OF MONEY

Sam was still uncomfortable with this information and slowly began to map out how the money flowed. He drew a diagram on the whiteboard in his office that showed that a hospitalist staffing company sought its profit by establishing itself as the de facto provider of patient care but at new (and higher) rates than the hospital could achieve on its own. The company had a national presence across many markets and hospitals and used that leverage to negotiate those higher rates.

The company charged the hospital for a portion of the salaries along with a management fee, which likely included not just the cost of the company's billing and collecting, but also the costs of the leadership development programming and medical directorships.

Sam estimated that if his current hospitalists could further reduce LOS and achieve better (and appropriate) documentation, the hospital could benefit by several million dollars.

Further, if the hospitalists could achieve those goals, Sam might have more bandwidth to approach the independent physicians and create structures (interdisciplinary rounds, tele-rounds, case management briefs, weekend huddles, etc.) that would help the independent doctors in their throughput of patient care and further save the hospital some money.

All told, Sam suspected that he could achieve the savings requested by the C-suite without resorting to outside contracting and loss of control and avoid the excess charges to the unsuspecting patients who were admitted to the out-sourced, independently run hospitalist service. To do that, he would need some additional managerial support, and that would be a tall order to ask of the C-suite.

Next, Sam called a meeting with some members of the finance team and asked for revenue projections under a few hypothetical models. Sam wanted to know what the revenue would look like if CMS paid the hospital based on a higher CMI, and if the efforts by the current hospitalists, given all of the "cases" under their care, could move the needle for the whole hospital CMI.

In other words, he wanted to know if 60% of the discharges were accomplished by the hospitalists and their documentation supported an appropriately higher CMI, would it be enough for the entire hospital CMI to move upward.

Sam also asked for revenue projections if the hospitalists moved other metrics, such as the HRRP and the "Communication with Doctors" domain of the HCAHPS. Would the hospital be in a position to achieve a higher star rating and what would the potential revenue look like?

Finally, if Sam brought in a VP-level administrator to oversee the hospitalists while Sam hired another physician advisor whose sole focus was to work with independent physicians (who managed 30-35% of the other medical admissions), what would those costs look like and how much revenue would be achieved as a result of the PA hire?

He also asked for an itemized amount of reimbursement (or removal of penalty) relative to any quality measure for which there was either a payment or a penalty associated with the individual measure, such as readmission reduction for CHF or COPD.

AN ALTERNATIVE SOLUTION

With all of those projections, Sam came up with a plan. He knew he could not match any profit sharing or stock compensation as offered by the staffing companies to its physicians, much less its training and development programs designed to produce highly skilled documentarians and throughput clinicians, but he could begin to offer hospitalists bonus incentives for achieving readmission reduction goals, HCAHPS scores, and CDI adherence.

Using the whiteboard again, he figured that mathematically the hospitalists could earn about 10% more in compensation if they "hit" each metric or target in total, and that the hospital would still stand to benefit from its gross revenues even after paying the physicians their bonus, hiring a VP, and utilizing another physician advisor.

Sam gathered his quality team and asked about the gaps that needed to close for the hospital to improve its CMS star rating from 3 to 4. He subsequently asked for a plan to do that with the various resources at his disposal, such as hospitalists and ED physicians. Sam held a private meeting with the CFO and shared his models under an improved CDI and higher star rating.

Finally, Sam was ready to speak to the C-suite. He made an elegant but brief presentation proposing to retain the current hospitalists and ED physicians, to redesign their contracts, and to pay the physicians with bonuses based on valuable metrics. In turn, he committed to a dollar amount by which the hospital would benefit in three years if everything went as planned.

As far as the ED group was concerned, they would remain independent; however, Sam offered a contract that paid for medical directorships and provided bonus dollars for performance metrics. His only requests were for a VP to monitor and track all of the results until the three-year period was concluded, along with a physician advisor to focus on the non-employed physicians. The CEO, COO, and CFO all signed off on the plan.

As part of his due diligence for the mission at hand, Sam learned that staffing companies were using predatory practices in an attempt to take their split of a bigger pie (i.e., out-of-network payments, which we will explore in Chapter 14).

Sam wanted more of the pie to remain at the hospital, to keep patients satisfied and well cared for, and to have loyal physicians at the end of the day.

He did not share his personal view on the matter (much less the information that led to his conclusions) with the C-suite. He knew that he was taking an extraordinary risk to his own professional career, but he also knew that the practice of hospital medicine needed to remain sacrosanct for the benefit of the patients, while keeping the institution on solid ground. One without the other was a recipe for problems related to patient care.

Sam asked himself the critical questions about who would benefit, who had the power to determine the outcomes, and what were the dangers involved. He exhibited tremendous leadership in establishing a strategic vision to ensure the right care team would be in place to provide the best possible care.

With limited resources, Sam had learned to stop boiling the ocean, but rather to simmer the pot and to achieve the same results. If anyone was going to split the money, it would be him and for the best possible outcomes given the circumstances.

Not surprisingly, the in-house physicians eventually caught wind of the outside agency meetings and C-suite deliberations. They began to worry about their own employment and future with Akron.

With the C-suite approval and new contracts in hand as employees of Akron City Medical Group, Sam held several town halls and group meetings with the hospitalist physicians whose contracts were up for renewal.

Sam provided ample time for questions and answers and as the physicians recognized that they could have been outsourced or re-hired under different management and that in addition to the normal wRVU structure, they could now earn a bonus for the hospital metrics, there was near universal acceptance of the new terms and Sam earned accolades from the physicians and the C-suite.

As for the independent ED physician group, the existing contract had been arranged primarily as an exclusivity agreement, but the hospital did pay a nominal amount of management dollars for the ED group to achieve desired outcomes, while the physician group managed its own billing and collections, for which they paid a fee to an outside company.

Sam offered to provide the same service but at a 30% reduction in the fee currently paid and to rebate a lump sum at the end of each quarter if the group achieved the new metrics. The group could take the lump sum and do whatever it pleased with it, but it would essentially amount to each physician receiving a bonus for the goals if the ED group chose to split up the money that way.

If things went this way, this contract cost would end up being net neutral for the hospital compared to the current contract (since the hospital was already paying for management activities), but if the ED physicians could achieve the desired goals, not only would the hospital revenue improve enough to cover the cost of billing/collecting that were fully rebated, the hospital would still stand to see substantial revenue.

LESSONS LEARNED

- Traditionally physicians are trained to be independent, critical thinking professionals and not employed/contracted labor. This creates tension now and will for the foreseeable future.
- Contracting for physicians has many subtleties, not the least of which is the financial structure. Beyond the contract, the alignment of goals and objectives is critical.
- In some cases, the physician leadership structure is much more of an imperative in working with contracted, employed physicians than simply having stated goals.

- Contingencies for staffing are important should economics shift and cause a change in the current physician employments in place at your organization.

QUESTIONS TO ASK

- Is it better to own and operate your own physician labor pool or contract with an outside company?
- How much due diligence is required when contracting with outside physician staffing companies?
- Can you work with your business office team to create a complete cost/revenue analysis of each and every employed physician, such as an Excel spreadsheet that displays each physician's coding/CDI, GMLOS, imaging utilization, etc.? Is converting each measurement to a dollar value a useful way to manage the labor pool?
- Is measuring the value of physicians antithetical to the art/practice of medicine? Or, in an era of limited resources and shrinking reimbursement, is it simply an imperative?
- Could it be possible that it is, in fact, more ethical to manage physicians who do not produce value and who waste money?
- Who speaks those truths about physician cost in your organization? And to whom? Who should own those conversations?
- Are you willing to terminate contracts with individual (or groups of) physicians if they are wasteful to your hospital, clinic, ASC, etc.?
- How many ways can you/should you "bonus" physicians over performance? What are the best metrics? How do you avoid "metric shaming?"
- How do you split up lump sum value payments in your clinic for top performance when the attribution is not because of a single physician, but rewarded for the team effort and organizational infrastructure?
- Can you avoid salary cuts for your employed physicians?

CHAPTER **14**

Social Contracting:
For-Profit/Not-for-Profit

"They are not customers. They are patients.
Do you know the origin of the word patient? It
is derived from French, which is derived from
Latin, *patiens*. And it means "to suffer."

J.G., MD, Board Trustee

DR. SOPHIA LIONTARI REACHED HER BREAKING POINT when she
met a patient who was discharged from a recent hospital stay and
was scheduled into her clinic for follow-up. Sophie walked into the
exam room and introduced herself to a 23-year-old woman named
Anne who was attending nursing school and who was also working
part-time as a waitress at a nice restaurant in town.

Anne had become progressively more fatigued in recent months
and blamed it on her work and school schedules. One night, while
serving a table of four, she felt dizzy enough that she almost spilled
her tray of entrees and the following day she nearly passed out in
her apartment when she got up after studying for two hours at her
computer.

Fortunately, her roommate was present, and she was able to ease
Anne to the sofa before she could injure herself. For the next 20-30
minutes, it appeared that Anne was unsteady and unable to function
without a strong sense of nearly passing out again, so her roommate,
who was also a nursing student, took Anne's vitals and found that
Anne was somewhat tachycardic and slightly hypotensive. She drove
Anne to the local ED for what they both believed was simple volume
depletion and orthostasis.

As part of the evaluation in the ED, a CBC was obtained which
revealed a hemoglobin of 9 with a hematocrit of 27. Her indices

151

suggested microcytic anemia, so Anne was offered a transfusion and placement into the observation unit.

When the hospitalist physician assigned to the observation unit was notified of Anne's placement, he went into the room and proceeded with a history and physical. He quickly learned that Anne had been experiencing intermittent abdominal pain, bloating, and diarrhea for several months, while at the same time, her menstruation was light and irregular at best.

Iron studies were ordered that night and the results in the morning revealed that Anne had classic iron deficiency anemia. After the transfusion, she felt significantly better and asked to be discharged. The physician ostensibly decided that light menstruation alone would not account for the iron deficiency, so he recommended a work-up for her GI symptoms.

Anne did not have insurance and did not have any meaningful way to cover all of the bills she knew she would receive. The hospitalist provided the name of a clinic for follow-up where she might be eligible for Medicaid (given her low income) and where she could be seen for regular care.

Anne called for an appointment and was scheduled for an appointment in four weeks. Within three weeks of the diagnosis of anemia, she experienced even more intense abdominal pain and presented again to the ED for evaluation. Once again, her CBC revealed a low hemoglobin and hematocrit. She was sent for an abdominal CT scan while still in the ED.

The imaging revealed multiple areas of bowel wall edema and inflammatory changes in the region of the terminal ileum, so she was admitted to an inpatient bed for further work-up along with another transfusion.

Anne felt so ill that she agreed to admission despite her lack of funds. After consultation with a GI, Anne underwent a colonoscopy and was started on oral iron, a short course of oral, delayed release budesonide, and a loading dose of adalimumab under the diagnosis of Crohn's ileitis.

After another few days of IV hydration, another transfusion, and a low-residue diet, Anne felt well enough for discharge and was instructed to seek follow-up care at the same clinic as recommended previously. It was at the clinic that she met Sophie.

CONSIDERING OPTIONS

When JMED needed to upgrade their EHR to best capture all of the financial opportunities related to VBP (and to ease the physician's burden of their previously clunky EHR system), Sophie decided on two things to reclaim some sense of control over her career trajectory.

While she loved the outpatient-only schedule, the clinic was terribly busy and had many different priorities (e.g., committees, productivity, meaningful use requirements, ACO requirements, etc.) and she felt as though she was no longer simply "free" to care for patients.

Volunteering

The first thing that she did was volunteer twice a month at the local federally qualified health center (FQHC) where she was neither compensated nor held to any productivity goal, and wherein she had sovereign immunity from any claims against any of her professional skills (i.e., medical malpractice claims). She felt much "freer" on the days in the FQHC clinic and enjoyed the atmosphere of caring for individuals who were in tough circumstances and who were also very appreciative of her compassion.

Learning the Business Side

The second thing that Sophie did was to enroll in an MBA program. She had decided to advance her business acumen and skills through a program at the local university to gain some mastery over the issues that were constantly surfacing at JMED.

This, too, felt personal and she was not exactly seeking more status or more responsibility, but she constantly felt inadequately prepared to meet the challenges of helping JMED achieve both its clinical and business goals.

With the support of her husband, she enrolled in a program that offered hybrid learning that was flexible for her work and family schedule. After just two years, she earned her master's degree in business.

A VIEW FROM THE FRONT-LINES OF INSURANCE

Sophie was recruited to serve as a medical director for a company that offered peer-to-peer support for clinicians seeking authorizations from commercial insurance companies. She remained curious about the "business" side of medicine and agreed to work for this company in a part-time capacity one day a week answering calls from physicians who were seeking authorizations.

It was agreed that Sophie could not take calls from anyone in JMED (or from the FQHC for that matter) and that she could only service authorization requests from physicians appealing to insurance companies that did not have contracts with JMED.

As part of the role, she would be sent to a series of training sessions to learn more about the payer side of healthcare delivery. While most of the training sessions were devoted to all of the parameters of authorization, prior authorization, peer-to-peer, denials, and appeals, Sophie learned that each insurance company had its own protocols and processes for their coverages.

Her job was to act as a clinical voice and to review the request for authorization in a peer-to-peer manner and to determine if the medical care that was requested was appropriate under the guidelines made available to her.

If requests fell outside of the guidance, Sophie, as a licensed physician, could render a decision for or against authorization, with appropriate justification for her decision. If the requesting physician disagreed, the physician could advance the request as an appeal to the insurance company medical director.

Sophie was, in effect, acting as a third-party intermediary between the front-line clinical provider and the payer for the care. Regardless of each insurance company's unique procedures, those procedures were generally similar, and they all had one thing in common: the medical loss ratio (MLR).

Medical Loss Ratio

The MLR has been around for several years but was heavily legislated with the passage of the ACA in 2012. Historically, the MLR represented the ratio, often expressed as a percentage, that an insurer "loses" from its premium income for administration costs, marketing, and profits.

Further, some (but not all) states put in place regulations that mandated how much of the premium dollars the insurers could "keep" and how much they had to spend on medical claims.

With the passage of the ACA, however, the MLR was federally defined as 80% for medium insurers and 85% for large insurers.[1] To illustrate the point, a large insurance company was required to spend 85% of its collected premium dollars on medical claims in the year under consideration. If it only spent 83% of its dollars, it had to rebate the 2% to the insured members (either directly, or to the employer, or as a split between employer/employee, or applied to the next year's expected premiums).

On the surface this appeared to be a very robust regulation that demanded that insurers not withhold payments for medical care to maximize their profits. On the other hand, the remaining "loss" representing the remaining 15% of the premium could be managed in an almost unfettered way.

By tightly organizing how much it spent on administrative costs and marketing, both of which make up the bulk of the remaining 15% after medical claims were paid, a company could increase profitability. Hence, outsourcing parts of the authorization processes such as with Sophie's new role, could reduce expenses within the accounting of the insurer and lead to an increase in profit.

Similarly, insurers could continue to sell their products to more employers and achieve a greater base of revenue from which to work with such that while the margin might not improve, the total revenue might.

Additionally, the timeliness of payments was not exactly regulated, so insurers did not rush the non-emergent processes and followed their lengthy authorization and appeals processes, which allowed them to seemingly benefit from holding onto the cash.

There were many unintended consequences of the legislated MLR; an excellent paper by Scott Harrington at UPenn's Wharton School of Business outlines many potential scenarios.[1]

Additionally, when the COVID pandemic struck, many insurers found themselves with tremendous amounts of retained premium dollars as the utilization for healthcare services dropped dramatically because of cancelled elective procedures, lockdowns, short staffing for services, and social distancing/patient deferrals. Those dollars equated to low MLRs due to less money spent on medical claims in 2020 that, under the ACA legislation, required that the insurers rebate tremendous amounts of money to the covered members.[2]

Within two years or so, the opposite occurred as pent-up demand created an overage of medical claims that exceeded the MLRs (upwards of 87%–89%) and caused insurers to hike premiums to maintain enough leftover cash after paying the increased claims to "hit" the target ratio of 85% for the next year.

In other words, medical loss ratios over 85% reduce the profits of the insurance company. The obvious recourse for the insurer would be to increase premiums in the next year rather than see a profit loss.

Finally, with the ACA, there was the added piece to the numerator that accounted for money the insurance company spent on quality improvement. Thus, insurers were incentivized to increase the amount of money devoted to "quality improvement" which is not necessarily the same as a paid claim, and, in a perverse manner, they could equally reduce the amount paid in claims so that the total numerator was still 85% of the premiums.

For more on the role of quality improvements that were accounted in the numerator, and other various elements of the MLR management, please read an excellent *Modern Healthcare* post (and its accompanied links) by Shelby Livingston, a reporter on the insurance industry.[3]

ECONOMICS OF FOR-PROFIT AND NOT-FOR-PROFIT ENTERPRISES

Despite her MBA, Sophie knew nothing about this structure until she started working for the intermediary authorization company. The MBA program taught her about economics and balance sheets, profit/loss, EBITA, and a number of other conventional concepts, but it did not unpack the intricate mechanisms of how insurance companies used protocols, procedures, and processes to meet legal requirements and to maintain its profitability out of the remaining 15%.

In other words, her degree did not elucidate how they split up all of those premium dollars into claims, administrative/quality improvement costs, and profits.

One key lesson that Sophie learned from her MBA program, however, centered on the economics of for-profit and not-for-profit enterprises and the distinction in relation to hospital-based organizations.

To complicate matters and despite the nomenclature, they both must generate profit to be sustainable. Oftentimes within hospital administrative meetings, the leadership refers to the profit as "margin," but it is also referred to as net operating income (NOI). NOI describes the revenue that is left over after accounting for expenses.

So, if it is true that both for-profit and not-for-profit organizations must generate profit (i.e., margin), what is the difference between the two?

In a for-profit healthcare structure, the entity is owned by investors, much like any other for-profit business. While for-profit healthcare organizations deliver health services, they aim to make a profit to satisfy the investors. They have a business-driven culture to achieve their fiduciary goals and to satisfy the shareholders/investors, some of whom sit on the system level board of trustees.

Not-for-profit entities are ostensibly owned by the public (and this is far more complex than it sounds) and (should) have service-driven cultures, as it is the responsibility of not-for-profit hospitals/health systems to provide health services without the intent of making a profit and they are accountable to their donors, community members, and other stakeholders for abiding by their stated missions.

What fundamentally separates the two types of models, however, is how the institution relates to the social contract of delivering healthcare to its community. If that contract exists to deliver a necessary and complex service, in this case healthcare, and to deliver it fairly, equitably, and competently, it is the obligation of society to ensure the structures and resources for its delivery.

As part of that conceptual contract, not-for-profit hospitals are afforded two primary elements that are materially different from for-profit facilities: (1) they are tax-exempt and (2) any profit/margin/NOI must be reinvested into the organization.

Additionally, and importantly, federal law requires that not-for-profit hospitals — which account for nearly three-fifths (58%) of community hospitals — provide some level of charity care as a condition of receiving tax-exempt status.[4]

How much care, who is eligible, the policies of such care, and how that uncompensated care (aka "bad debt") is paid for depends on many local factors and in large part on state rules and regulations.

Further, and not always apparent to those unfamiliar with hospital environments and the societal relationship (i.e., contract), when a not-for-profit hospital is sold, any profit from the sale is returned to the community from which the structure originated.

This can mean that not-for-profit hospital sales can become political hot potatoes between local community leaders and those with other interests. This tension is evident today, especially in rural areas that are struggling financially and where the community may be divided about how best to manage the financially flailing institution as a piece of infrastructure that needs support for the medically underinsured or underserved versus an asset that could enrich the community budgets if it were to be sold at a profit (more on that in Chapter 15).

Federally Qualified Health Centers

The FQHC has its origins in the Public Health Service Act of 1944, which provided a legislative basis for the provision of public health services in the United States, and is funded under the Health Center Consolidation Act (Section 330 of the Public Health Service Act) of 1996.[5]

An FQHC is a community-based organization that provides comprehensive primary care and preventive care to persons of all ages, regardless of their health insurance status or ability to pay, and therefore are a critical component of the healthcare safety net.

FQHCs operate under a consumer board of directors governance structure and under the supervision of the Health Resources and Services Administration (HRSA), which is part of the United States Department of Health and Human Services (HHS).

FQHCs generally stand as clinic/outpatient sites of care and originally were meant to provide comprehensive health services to the medically underserved to reduce the patient load on hospital emergency rooms.

Under both the Bush and Obama administrations, however, the centers were expanded to enhance primary care services in under-served urban and rural communities, particularly for the underinsured and uninsured, along with migrant workers and non-U.S. citizens.

FQHCs can charge for services on a sliding-fee scale based on patients' family income and size. In return for serving all patients regardless of ability to pay, the centers receive federal government cash grant dollars, cost-based reimbursement for their Medicaid patients, and malpractice coverage under the Federal Tort Claims Act.[5]

Even with those benefits, the clinics are constantly challenged to manage their costs and to identify pathways for Medicaid eligibility of their patients to keep their expenses and revenues balanced and maintain operations.

One method of managing costs is to allow providers such as Sophie to periodically serve on a volunteer basis and with a degree of malpractice indemnification/immunity, and without any professional compensation.

Support for Rural Hospitals

As a corollary to the FQHCs, hospitals that have a substantial proportion of their revenue from government sources (i.e., large Medicare payer percentage), such as rural hospitals, may qualify for a set of unique payment structures that are nicely outlined by The Rural Health Information Hub (RHIhub), launched in December 2002 as the national clearinghouse of the Federal Office of Rural Health Policy.[6]

As an example, akin to the early hospital days of the 1930s and 1940s (recall Chapter 2), one such program, the Rural Community

Hospital Demonstration, provides cost-based reimbursement.[6] The program is designed to assess the impact of cost-based reimbursement on the financial viability of small rural hospitals and test for benefits to the community.

These hospitals often have much higher costs than those that are part of large health systems with tremendous buying power for lower cost supplies, pharmaceuticals, etc., and without adequate private reimbursement to make up for the shortfall in payments by Medicare, often run at a financial loss. The program is set up to reimburse eligible hospitals for the costs of their materials and goods in an attempt to avoid such heavy operating costs.

ADDRESSING GAPS IN THE SOCIAL CONTRACT OF HEALTHCARE

It is important to recognize that not-for-profit institutions, FQHC sites, rural hospitals, and the medical loss ratio all have one thing in common: the structural and legislated requirement to provide for services (and claims in the case of the MLR) under the implicit social contract of healthcare in exchange for specific protected fiduciary benefits: tax exemption, federal cash grants, cost based reimbursement, or the right to determine "profitability" after care has been rendered.

When Sophie met Anne in the clinic after Anne's second discharge, Anne was feeling marginally better but needed several things to continue to improve: the delayed-release oral budesonide, adalimumab self-injectable pens, a GI referral, regular labs, help for the oral iron constipation, and possibly B12 injections.

Sophie immediately encountered multiple issues for Anne such as who is responsible for the consultant referral fees and for the cost of medication. Sophie wondered about the role of the hospital and whether or not it bore some responsibility for the costs of the continuity of care.

Who was ultimately responsible and what, if anything, could Sophie do about any of it? Her MBA did not prepare her for these questions related to the gaps in the so-called social contract of healthcare.

Sophie cared for Anne that day to the best of her ability, made all of the necessary arrangements, and told her husband when she got home that she had reached her professional breaking point and wanted something different for herself. She wanted to pivot and work full time in the payer universe. She believed that there was a better way to ensure that individuals could have the care that they deserved and to have those costs reasonably covered as to each individual's circumstance.

She would still volunteer for the FQHC, but she wanted to learn for herself how systems could better organize around the costs of care for the benefit of the patient. She applied to become a regional CMO at a newly created, clinically integrated network of medical groups formed to meet the needs of the future of care delivery known as "population health."

LESSONS LEARNED

- The social contract of delivering healthcare to a society creates an inseparable relationship between government and the providers and recipients of healthcare.
- As such, local, state, and federal structures all play a role in the splitting up of the healthcare dollar.
- With tax revenues as a generic basis, government plays a role in the distribution of dollars toward the delivery of care through direct payment (fee-for-service, value-based payment, bundled payment) or indirectly through structural entitlements (tax-exemptions, grants, expanded Medicaid offerings).

QUESTIONS TO ASK

- Should the MLR be regulated by the federal government or by individual states based on local economics?
- What might happen if MLR was unregulated?
- Should insurance companies be allowed to have processes that delay the authorization functions? If 80-85% of premiums must be paid on claims, who regulates the validity of claims?

- Are prior authorizations a tactic to justifiably spend premium dollars only on the "right care" based on standards/guidelines or an allowable process to invalidate claims/delay claims/hold claims to manage hitting the sweet spot of 80-85% MLR?
- Why are there individuals who are uninsured/underinsured in the United States?
- How does the gap in healthcare coverage impact the design of individual healthcare delivery systems (local clinics, hospitals, etc.)?
- What is the role of CMO regarding the social contract of health in the United States?
- Should not-for-profit hospitals create care models to cover the immediate costs of discharges (prescriptions, referrals, durable medical equipment) for the underinsured/uninsured in addition to their requirement to pay for inpatient charity care? If not, who should cover those transitional costs for that population until the patient reaches a clinic?
- Is it fair that an employed doctor be paid (under an wRVU contract) for uncompensated care when the hospital does not receive reimbursement under a for-profit model? What about under a not-for-profit model when the hospital is supposed to provide "charity care?"
- Is there value to investing in the transitions of care that occur with patients with complex medical conditions? Value to whom?
- Where can CMOs find and/or create value in the fractured components of healthcare payments?

CHAPTER 15

Financing It All

"Capital is that part of wealth which is
devoted to obtaining further wealth."

Alfred Marshall, English economist,
author of *Principles of Economics*

WHEN DR. HENRY "PUFF" BALLARD turned 60, long before his
dementia diagnosis, he decided it was time to purchase a boat for
cruising along Lake Ontario. With 30 years of practice under his belt,
his children grown and out on their own, and a stable practice, he
believed that he had earned the right to a little free time, and boating
was his dream.

Over the years he had been rather prudent and managed his
expenses close to his revenues, with the ability to pay off his mortgage and establish a modest savings account that he would draw on,
along with Social Security, whenever he decided to retire.

In practice, whenever he needed to re-supply his office with
splints, suture material, needles, syringes, and various other sundries
required to care for his patients, he had the office manager pay for
the materials from the practice bank account, just like you would
an ordinary household.

In those days, Puff never worried about having enough available
cash to meet all of the needs of the practice, including the office payroll and supply requirements. When he considered the boat, however,
he decided to seek a loan rather than dip into his personal savings
account, which was bundled into certificates of deposit (CDs).

When he met with the loan officer at Lockport Regional Bank,
the entire process took about 30 minutes. The loan officer had been
a patient of Dr. Ballard for many years, as had the loan officer's family. The loan officer knew that Dr. Ballard had paid off the mortgage
that Lockport Regional Bank held on his home and could not only

post a variety of assets (the house, the practice, savings account/CDs, etc.) as collateral for the loan, but since Dr. Ballard wasn't planning to retire any time soon, he had a steady income from which to make the loan re-payments.

In 1976, when Puff requested his loan for the purchase of his dream boat, average interest rates on 30-year fixed mortgages were around 8.8%. Ordinarily, the bank would offer a modest loan to a customer for about 10% during this time, but the loan officer, given the longstanding relationship (both personal and business) that existed between them, offered Puff a 60-month loan of $5,000 at 8%. For this, Puff would pay the bank just over $100/month until the loan was fully repaid.

If Puff did this for the full length of the loan, he would have paid the bank about $1,000 in interest payments, in addition to the principle (borrowed amount) of the original $5,000, and, in effect, paid $6,000 for his boat.

At the end of the five years, why would Puff pay more than the sales cost for the boat? Because at the time, assuming interest rates stayed the same, his interest-earning CDs totaling $50,000, if left untouched, would balloon to $63,800 and earn him much more money (even adjusted for inflation) than the amount paid in interest payments on the boat.

In effect, Puff put his money "to work" against the "cost of capital" to finance the boat and would end up with a bigger nest egg and his dream boat. If he pulled $5,000 out of the CDs, he would only end up with $57,400 after five years.

Now, at first, it would appear that under either circumstance, he would have "spent" about $6,400 ($63,800 – $57,400) on the boat; however, the scenario that avoids dipping into the CDs leads to even greater savings in another five years, given the compounding interest of the higher balance ($63,800 turns into $81,400, while $57,000 turns into only $73,000).

The final challenge he had to face was how to actively manage the monthly $100 loan payment. He could pay for the loan each month from his regular income or withdraw it from cash in his savings account each month, hoping to impact his compound growth only marginally.

He started with the former plan, but as interest rates rose over the next five years, reaching close to 14% when the boat was fully paid off, he pulled out enough cash to close the loan and pushed $100/month over into the CDs in order to grow his nest egg, which eventually reached $163,000 in 1986. By the time he found out he had dementia, it was $236,000, even with all of the interest rate changes during that era. In 1992, that amount of money is about the same as $550,000 in today's economy.

Not too bad for old Puff, a simple country doctor who figured out a way to leverage his assets, borrow against them, making both the borrowed capital and earned capital work for him to accumulate more assets and grow more wealth. And, if he so chose, he could continue to replicate the cycle of leveraging, borrowing, and accumulating for as long as he was able.

PAYING TO PRACTICE HEALTHCARE

As we have learned, the growth of medical care in the United States created structures that moved money in a variety of ways: practice management, billing/collection, administrative costs, etc. And, as the complexities grew, these ever-increasing structures also grew, although many did not generate revenue. They consumed dollars to capture dollars that were flowing along the spectrum from payer to provider, taking splits and shares along the way.

Also, in terms of medical facilities, devices, procedures, infusion centers, dialysis centers, etc., we have learned that the more those things are used via large volumes of care, the more fees and revenue were garnered for the stakeholders.

In the case of utilization producing revenue, though, those medical "things" commanded such large price tags that they could not be paid for out of practice revenue, which was already stretched for the daily operating costs (salaries, supplies, utilities, etc.).

We have also seen the increase in costly transformational health system requirements, some of which generate partial revenue (physician employment), create savings or optimize efficiency (case management), or aid in documentation and charge capture (information technology).

These latter items may or may not be cost-neutral, but they also have very large price tags associated with them and require capital to keep them going.

Hospitals' potential to raise capital depends largely on whether they are for-profit or not-for-profit, and whether they are single facilities or part of larger networks. However, all hospitals need available capital, and they have to be fiscally responsible for the "cost" of the capital. Likewise, all integrated health systems, along with large stand-alone medical groups and insurers, also need capital for their enterprise.

For the purposes of this chapter, we are going to review the essence of how hospitals manage their requirements; in the lessons/questions at the end, you will be able to apply the principles to whatever system you embrace.

Generating Capital

For-profit hospitals select from a variety of resources to generate capital, and those hospitals that are part of larger networks have even greater opportunities. Suffice to say, the main resources are either through bank credit and borrowing or through equity in the form of shares and stocks.

For example, a small for-profit hospital system has five hospitals and wishes to build a sixth hospital containing about 100 beds. Prior to the COVID-19 pandemic, it would have cost about $100 million to do so (est. $1 million/bed). Generally, the hospital system would have hard assets such as its current buildings, some of which were paid for and others with loans to be paid off.

Perhaps one of the hospitals was acquired and the system pays a lease on the property. Further, the system likely has investments in stocks and bonds that have value and/or generate returns. And, finally, the system may have a line of credit from a large banking institution that makes money available for payroll and vendor obligations.

When the board of trustees authorizes plans for the new hospital, they are, in effect, fulfilling their fiduciary responsibility and both trusting and allowing the C-suite to obtain the funding for the new building without adversely affecting the overall system.

At this point, the CFO most likely holds meetings with banks and lending institutions to secure a loan. While the system may already have an adequate line of credit, as described above, a loan would be different in its obligations and interest rates. The interest rate on a line of credit is quite different from that required for a single loan that will require a long-term re-payment plan.

With the same caution as displayed by the loan officer in Lockport, the lending bank must establish the hospital system's ability to re-pay the loan, which in turn, will determine the interest rate on the loan.

If the hospital system's financial history is positive, the hospital will hopefully get a favorable interest rate, and at $100 million, every percentage point or fraction thereof translates into hundreds of thousands, if not millions, of dollars to be paid back to the bank.

For those of you who know all about balance sheets, this may seem as rudimentary as assets and liabilities, but for the average aspiring CMO, it is likely that these areas were never addressed in medical school, residency, and practice prior to becoming an executive.

The balance sheet issue is far less important here than the concept that a hospital will have a wide range of financial support mechanisms to pay staff, purchase supplies, and fund its entire enterprise, and that every CMO ought to be mindful of what is happening in the finance office, as each/every decision that the CMO makes could very well impact those mechanisms.

STOCKS, BONDS, AND ADDITIONAL FUNDING

As part of that support structure, there are various obligations that the finance team must meet regularly to maintain the organization's financial health. Other methods of funding new hospital construction include government grants/loans, philanthropy, bonds, and private investment. In this chapter we will talk about bonds; in the next chapter we will learn about private investment.

Issuing Stocks

If we expand our hypothetical FP hospital system to include 40 hospitals, we will see a system well-positioned and large enough to raise money in the equity market system by issuing common stock that can be bought and sold in an exchange such as the New York Stock Exchange.

Simply put, the hospital leadership can work with underwriters who will determine the value of the system ("company") and support a plan to issue stock which can be bought and sold by brokers and ultimately by shareholders.

For a specified dollar amount, almost anyone can own shares in a publicly traded company and can, in turn, buy or sell more of those shares, depending on the goals of making a profit or spreading out a loss.

To continue with the hypothetical hospital's finance, we assume the company has been paid for the stock certificates and has realized a significant profit from the underwriter's offering. Now, instead of carrying debt on a bank loan, the hospital system is at the mercy of the shareholders, some of whom may be sitting on the board of trustees.

Shareholders seek a return on their investment, which may be in the form of a quarterly dividend paid by the company (and may/may not reflect the company's profits); however, the return today may be seen in the rising value of the stock on the exchange based on the financial health of the hospital company.

Refer to the stock symbol HCA, to see how Hospital Corp. of America Healthcare, Inc. has fared since its inception as a publicly traded company. An investor who bought the stock at $25 in 2012 could now sell it for just over 10 times that amount at $289. Imagine if Puff's widow or children had put the $236,000 accumulated in 1992 into investments that kept pace with inflation ($385,000) and then bought HCA stock in 2012. It would be worth nearly $4.5 million today.

Our hypothetical company issued stock which resulted in a sizeable amount of cash, allowing them to expand their facility footprint.

Issuing Bonds

Not-for-profit hospitals, which make up 60% of the U.S. hospital environment, on the other hand, cannot share ownership with individuals or groups; therefore, they are unable to participate in stock issues to raise capital.

Instead, not-for-profit hospitals mostly use bonds or occasionally levy taxes on local communities and, in my opinion, find themselves in an even trickier situation than for-profit hospitals that are dealing with shareholders.

If we return to our simple hypothetical hospital system, but change it to not-for-profit, and it is looking for $100 million to build a new facility, the leadership will work with several entities to raise the money through a bond issuance. In this circumstance, the bond will be a debt obligation such that in return for $100 million, the hospital company will pay the holders of the bond a percentage of the borrowed amount, similar to any type of loan.

Just as Puff had to pay back the bank 5% for his small loan, the hospitals will pay the bondholder an interest, "coupon rate," on the principal amount.

For this to occur, the hospital leadership must do two things, perhaps in parallel with each other: (1) they must either share or establish their credit rating through a company such as Moody's or Fitch and (2) they must work with the local municipality.

For convenience we will start with the credit rating. Leadership will invite one or more rating agencies to audit the hospital finances and to review all of its ongoing revenues and expenditures and determine if the hospital system has enough discretionary cash (and/or operating income) to pay the bondholder the percentage involved.

The agency will also determine other elements of the hospital business regarding hard assets and other collateral should the hospital be unable to pay its obligations. These types of audits will also influence the bond amount and what percentage will be paid.

The hospital cannot, however, actually put forth the bond. That is typically done with the local municipality. It is the local government that issues the general revenue bond, more commonly referred to as a municipal bond. The municipality, along with the bond agency, then arranges to have the bond sold to buyers such as brokers or fund managers.

Individual investors often prefer municipal bonds in that any interest income is earned without being subjected to federal (and often local/state) taxation.

Compared to stocks, the risk involved with bonds is much more connected to the hospital's ability to pay the monthly obligation to the bondholder. On the other hand, since bonds are often bought and sold in the secondary market, any gain realized at that time will be treated as a capital gain, while the underlying interest income is tax-free.

IMPACT IN THE GREATER COMMUNITY

Regardless of the economics of stocks and bonds in the marketplace, it is the municipality that is usually at the epicenter of the financial structure with a not-for-profit hospital bond. If the hospital cannot make its obligatory payments, the city could force the sale of the hospital to satisfy the bond and free itself from the bond obligation.

While the default rate on hospital-municipal bonds is historically low, municipalities are heavily impacted when a hospital struggles to make its payments on the bond. Banks and other investors tighten the credit to the hospital itself as well as to the municipality seeking to develop and expand other infrastructure projects that support the growth and business development of the community, such as airports and utilities.

When the bond is downgraded due to poor hospital financial performance, the less-tangible element is the decline of the hospital's and the community's reputation in the eyes of the public and of outside investors in the community.

As we have discussed often in this primer, hospitals play a critical role in the economic development of the community. Robust cities attract employers who need workers, who ultimately need healthcare and solid insurance benefits offered by those employers. This growth generates a property tax base for the city to fund institutions like schools and law enforcement, and to support other infrastructure projects through municipal bonds.

For example, Blount Memorial Hospital, an independent not-for-profit facility in Tennessee, faced financial difficulties to the point of a strained relationship with county leaders. County commissioners declared that Blount Memorial had an annual loss of more than $11 million and was in default of some bond obligations, all of which put some of Blount County's assets, as well as its credit ranking, at risk. There were real fears that the hospital would close critical services, or close altogether, to manage the financial woes.

The county sought alternative arrangements to ensure that the hospital would remain open and accessible. Blount Memorial leadership and the county officials had contentious discussions. The hospital filed lawsuits regarding who had rightful ownership, fiduciary control, and authority for hospital governance.

The Blount Memorial CEO, a physician turned executive, worked hard to maintain responsibility for the activities of the hospital and to provide healthcare for the community it served, while county officials believed that the hospital would benefit from a stronger regional hospital partnership to maintain basic access and services for the local community, all of which were threatened by the financial woes of the hospital.

Ultimately, the CEO resigned under substantial pressure and the two sides agreed to mediation that, at the time of this writing, has led to the use of a consulting firm to search for a viable partner that would ensure Blount Memorial would continue to provide care to the community.[1-3]

DEMONSTRATING FISCAL RESPONSIBILITY

When Dr. Sam Monroe found a way to maintain the employment contracts for the hospitalists and the agreements for the ED physicians that would hopefully maintain cost neutrality and possibly increase the overall payments to City Hospital, he was completely unaware that the C-suite had been in discussion about building a free-standing ED or an ambulatory surgery center about 30 miles away, with the potential for a new hospital as well.

Whether or not the physician contract initiative brought to Sam's attention regarding lowering the physician contracting expenses (or ultimately increasing overall hospital revenue) was framed in the larger financial goals of the hospital profitability, any positive impact from the re-contracting also served the larger goal of demonstrating financial responsibility and offered an attractive view for rating agencies and auditors.

By incrementally supporting the profit/loss balance of the hospital, Sam also supported the ability of leadership, inclusive of the board of trustees, to foster even more outreach for the hospital's larger community mission.

LESSONS LEARNED

- Hospitals and health systems have financial obligations that place pressure on the direction of the business and models of care.
- Hospitals and health systems, especially not-for-profit systems, are intricately bound to the fabric of the economic development of the communities that they serve.
- Awareness of how things work behind the scenes can have a material impact on how certain decisions are made or not made.
- Every healthcare executive should be observant of the unspoken financial forces that may affect the direction of the organization.
- Hospitals are not a limitless source of cash; even if they have healthy cash flows, they may need to seek additional funding to expand services.

QUESTIONS TO ASK

- A CMO should attempt to spend time with the CFO and learn about the types of obligations and responsibilities they must manage. What pressures exist on the profit/loss summaries and balance sheets? What financial obligations must the organization meet?

- What are the short-/medium-/long-term financial goals of the organization? Is there a need to pay off debt? To seek better credit ratings? To raise more capital?
- If your hospital has bonds held in the marketplace, what are they rated? What is the coupon rate? What do they yield? Does the secondary market play any role in creating new hospital bonds? What if the "bond market" is selling off?
- What does the board believe is in the best financial interest of the organization? Of the community? Where do shareholders fit into the strategic planning process?
- What type of relationships exist between the C-suite and community leaders? Should the CMO be part of those relationships? Why? Why not?
- Where do you see yourself within the finances of your organization? Do you want to become a subject matter expert? If so, is now a suitable time to seek an MBA rooted in healthcare economics?
- If you don't wish to be an expert, who can you partner with to stay abreast of financial impacts on your organization without also being a burden or distraction to their daily responsibilities? Do you simply need a crash course on how to read a balance sheet or profit/loss summary to stay current in meetings?

CHAPTER 16

Private Equity and Venture Capital

"You must spend money to make money."

—Titus Maccius Plautus (254 BC–184 BC), Roman playwright, poet, and philosopher

Dr. Sophie Liontari was hired as a regional CMO for an up-and-coming company that saw an opportunity to pull disparate elements together to deliver higher quality care for more individuals and with greater profitability.

One of her former colleagues always chided her for obtaining her MBA, saying, "So now that you have your MBA, are you talking with the bankers about the LIBOR today"? For reference, the London Inter-Bank Offered Rate (LIBOR) was the interest rate average calculated from estimates submitted by the leading banks in London about what each bank would be charged were it to borrow from other banks. It was the primary benchmark for short-term interest rates around the world until it was phased out at the end of 2021.[1]

Sophie's colleague was being snarky, but the point was that now that Sophie had an MBA, she had a new language around banking and might be well-equipped to navigate and negotiate with lenders.

When healthcare CFOs spend time seeking new credit or loan opportunities, it helps to know how the other side makes its money and how to pin down an interest rate that benefits both parties. Knowing where the bank stands to make money when lending its deposits sets the stage for how much to borrow and at what rate.

In contrast, in the world of private equity (PE), PE is exactly that: private. It is derived from capital that is invested into a company by a private equity firm (often one that specializes in investment

175

management), a venture capital fund, or an angel investor, which is a single entity with significant wealth.

Each category of investor has specific financial goals, management preferences, and investment strategies for profiting from their investments. Each category provides "working capital" to the target company to finance the company's development of new products and services.

With the capital comes equity (oftentimes in the form of private stock ownership) that is held privately and not traded on an open exchange. With equity comes influence on the structuring or restructuring of company operations, management, and, in some cases, formal control and ownership of the company. Similar to publicly traded company stock, the value of the equity investment rises and falls, depending on the financial performance of the company.

Further, private equity funds are bundled investment portfolios that specialize in bringing working capital to distressed companies. These funds are actively managed to garner positive results for their investor-clients.

Unlike PE that seeks more established companies in need of assistance, venture capital (VC) is a form of private equity financing that is provided to startup, early-stage, and emerging companies that have high growth potential. Similar to PE, VC firms invest in these early-stage companies in exchange for equity or an ownership stake.

Venture capitalists tend to take on the risk of financing fledgling startups in the hopes that some of the companies they support will become successful, but because startups face high uncertainty, VC investments have high rates of failure.

Ultimately VC investors want to establish an "exit" strategy to reap the benefits of the investment, such as the startup company selling shares to the public for the first time in an initial public offering (IPO), or disposing of shares via a merger or a sale to another buyer, such as another PE firm, a competitor company, or any other qualified structure with the means to buy the start-up.

Regardless of the investment strategies, PE and VC are not subject to the same public disclosures that we see with the traditional banking industry or open stock markets.

Sophia's new company had its roots in the insurance industry and, similar to the early HMOs described in Chapter 3, believed that it had a model that would effectively deliver superior care at a lower cost than in prior decades.

VERTICAL INTEGRATION: THE NEW FRONTIER

When the early HMOs were launched, they sought to control spending and guard against higher expenses and higher premiums. By cultivating narrow networks, capitation, and limited choices, the HMOs were "supply side" controllers of services for a single payer.

In recent years, a new paradigm, known as vertical integration, has emerged as the next frontier of the evolving space of healthcare delivery.

In the early days of the modern industrial revolution, vertical integration appeared as companies like Ford Motor Company sought ways to own raw materials, produce their own equipment and machinery, construct their products, and deliver, warehouse, distribute, and sell their final product to the consumer.

Today, healthcare, at least on paper, is a fragmented landscape of disparate elements all focused on the delivery of a product or service to restore or improve one's health and, as such, has been ripe for vertical integration for some time.

During the past several decades, insurance companies have grown in size and scale and have continued to seek ways to run more efficiently, waste fewer dollars, and deliver a product with affordable premiums to companies that offer employer-sponsored health plan benefits.

With the advent of electronic health records, improved claims management systems, and incredible computing power never before available, companies can mine data and perform analytics to look at high-cost services as well as the high utilizers of services and everything in between. With any luck, the payers are able to identify better pathways to increase the value of the care delivered and to affect the expenditures of someone in need of those services much earlier in the journey.

Further, the National Committee for Quality Assurance (NCQA), an independent nonprofit organization that works to improve healthcare quality through the administration of evidence-based standards, measures, programs, and ultimately voluntary accreditation, was established in 1990 as a means to improve the quality of the health insurance industry.[2] It does so, in part, by working with policymakers, employers, doctors, and patients, as well as health plans, to ensure that there are standards and measures by which to hold insurance companies accountable.

Health plans seek accreditation and measure performance through the administration and submission of the Healthcare Effectiveness Data and Information Set (HEDIS) elements. CMS requires that HMOs submit Medicare HEDIS data as part of the Medicare Advantage initiative. As such, insurers that offer commercial products and already have tools in place for HEDIS measurements can expand into offerings for MA health plans and continue to grow their revenue.

All of this translates into an incredible data-driven ecosystem wherein insurers are incentivized to collect data for their internal capabilities and business goals, and to meet external requirements to maintain market presence. Those same leading insurers depend on the physician-provider network(s) to deliver the care to meet the data requirements.

In theory, this type of collaboration is designed to improve the quality and outcomes of care that is paid for. While the government's goal is not profitability, the private sector goal is very much about its own business success and sustainability.

With Sophie's experience as a physician, as a leader in her medical group, as a medical director for a payer, and now with an MBA, she was well-positioned to take on the role of regional CMO of the new company. Aside from getting to know her executive peers and the new company's culture and mission, Sophie's first scope of responsibility was to help the CFO acquire primary care practices in the region that would serve as the base provider network for the larger company initiatives. Sophie was to evaluate practice valuations provided by outside consulting firms, review practice patterns of productivity and utilization, and assess adherence to best practices, to name a few tasks, all to determine if the acquisitions made rational clinical sense and were aligned with the company strategy.

Some executives were tasked with the operational pieces of acquisition (i.e., software, EHRs, ancillary services, staffing models, etc.) while others were to assemble various internal processes and pathways to guide clinical care and outcomes.

Additionally, there was a working group to map out every available value-based payment model offered by CMS and other payers and to embed technology into workflows to maximize revenue from every available source.

By using its own proprietary claims/payment information for patients enrolled in their health plan(s), the company could extrapolate the data and export the same methodologies for the providers to deliver care to patients under other health plans and with the same level of efficiency and clinical and economic outcomes. This would give the company added leverage when negotiating contract payment rates with other insurers, since they had their own internal proven track record to stand on.

The company poured tremendous resources into the technology needed to keep up with the clinical demands and practice growth. This required regular decisions about revenue, expenses, cash flow, and operating capital. Sophie was invited to participate in some of the meetings, particularly when the conversations linked clinical outcomes to the financial forecasting of the company.

When any discussion turned toward population health, Sophie was keenly interested in the notion of creating a scaffold around entire communities in an effort to deliver upstream and midstream interventions that would reap long-term health benefits and cost savings. But despite her knowledge and experience, she didn't think to ask about the sources of the company funding or to seek an invitation to any of the board's finance sub-committee or executive sub-committee meetings where she might have learned more about the inner workings of the company.

She was delighted to be part of something new, innovative, and comprehensive in the care delivery space that had previously frustrated her. The medical practices that the company acquired would be equipped to deliver comprehensive care and to meet the requirements of the insurers, all to the company's benefit.

She believed that the company was well positioned to create a digital health ecosystem that crossed over between payers and providers in an effort to improve the health of the community. This form of integration involving multiple payers (private and public) and providers was on a scale not seen since the early days of HMOs, and was increasingly more complex, yet still fragmented in some regards.

PE CASE STUDY: GROWTH OF A BUSINESS

Herbert Haft, born in Baltimore, Maryland, four years after Henry "Puff" Ballard, received a BS in pharmacy from George Washington University and later worked as a pharmacist at a local drug store. Haft and his wife opened their own drug store, Dart Drug, in 1955, offering drugs at a discount. This was at a time during which 70% of employed Americans were covered by an employer-sponsored health plan and a year before the famous AMA poll found that 43% of patients thought their doctor charged too much.[3]

Haft's timing was impeccable and the conditions were ripe to build a small empire of discount drug stores. That empire revolved around a simple business model of low pricing to attract large numbers of customers (self-pay or insured, or both through co-pay), and through the volume of sales, even with low margin, the business would succeed based on the large quantity of sales.

Haft extended his knack for this concept to a company called Crown Books, which also benefited from a discounted product/large sales model.[4]

The Hafts had three sons, one of whom, Robert, was educated at Harvard, served briefly in the U.S. Marine Corps, and who later worked in the family business under the label of The Dart Group, which included the discount drug store business.[5] Robert came to understand the business of selling discounted drugs and in 1995 bought a bankrupt discount drug store chain known as Phar-Mor.[6]

Phar-Mor was distressed as a result of one of the largest embezzlement cases and auditing frauds (at that time) by its founders, which led to the favorable purchase price by Robert (i.e., private equity). After Phar-Mor's subsequent dissolution in 2002, Robert founded and grew Vitamins.com, which had internet, retail, and catalog operations, along with some healthcare businesses.

In 1997, he founded Morgan Noble Healthcare Partners, a private equity company that invests in healthcare services and healthcare technology, and which has subsequently invested in companies like Captify Health, Carestream Health, and Privia Healthcare (founded in 2007), the physician enablement company we discussed in Chapter 11.[6]

By 2012, Privia was supported by institutional investors and private investors. One institutional investor, a New York-based private equity firm known as Health Enterprise Partners, which focused its investments on healthcare information technology and service businesses, was backed by some of the nation's leading health systems and plans, including Baylor Health Care System, Dignity Health, Riverside Health Care System, Sentara Healthcare, Sutter Health, UPMC, and WellPoint.[7]

Privia's individual investors are also healthcare industry leaders, including Robert Haft, who at the time also was the majority shareholder of Ambient Healthcare, Frank Williams, executive chairman of The Advisory Board Company and CEO of Evolent Health, and John Deane, CEO of Southwind, a division of The Advisory Board Company and one of the nation's leading physician practice management services for health systems.[7]

In 2021, Privia Healthcare went public and closed its initial IPO with $131 million raised.[7] In 2022, Goldman Sachs Group, a leading global financial institution, held 28 million shares or approximately 26% of company stock (i.e., ownership), which decreased slightly in 2023 to 24.8 million shares and just under 22% of ownership.[8]

Privia Healthcare is a solid example of a large company that serves thousands of physicians, and perhaps hundreds of thousands of patients, backed by a variety of capital sources, both private and public. Without that access to capital, it is hard to believe that such a company would exist today.

INTERSECTION OF TECHNOLOGY, INSURANCE, AND CAPITAL

Private equity is not interested only in the highly integrated, technology-driven medical practices of the United States; it is also interested in the insurance side of the care equation. Technology disrupts many industries, and health insurance is no exception.

As MA plans have become more available and adopted (as of this writing over half of all senior citizens are enrolled in privatized MA plans) new services have cropped up to market the plans, enroll Medicare beneficiaries in the plans, and assist in their administrative details.

One service that had existed for a long time in the form of insurance brokers, saw an untapped market in MA enrollment. Like in other industries, especially in the auto-home-casualty insurance marketplace, brokers bring customers and insurance products together for the right price and the right coverage and protections. These brokers earn money in the form of a commission from the initial sale of the policy or by collecting ongoing fees/dividends for the longitudinal renewal and payments made by policyholders, or both.

The market appeared so lucrative at its onset that Bain Capital, a private investment firm founded in part by Sen. Mitt Romney, invested $150 million into the MA brokerage space.[9]

With millions of seniors poised to convert or to initially enroll in MA plans, and with 5,000 U.S. citizens turning 65 each day and becoming eligible for Medicare, the "market" also had longevity built right in. Private insurers would be seeking enrollees and brokers could serve a tremendous need to match seniors to the right plans for their needs.

Another example of the intersection of today's technology, the world of health insurance, and capital to fund it, is Oscar Health, a company launched in 2012, just two years after the ACA was signed into law and just about two years before the exchange marketplace and individual mandates were enacted.[10]

With the support of multiple private investors (both PE and VC), first starting out with seed money from VC firm Thrive Capital, and later at least $30 million in funding by Peter Thiel's Founders Fund, Oscar Health went public and raised a staggering $1.2 billion on March 3, 2021, after an IPO.[10]

In 2014, its first year of providing health plans, Oscar Health had 16,000 members; in 2023, it reported having 1.1 million members across its platform, which equates to 1 in 13 ACA exchange-based enrollees.[10]

The internet-based platform allows people to research the various plan offerings and to determine benefits, individual costs (deductibles, co-pays, co-insurance), available physicians and hospitals, medication formularies, and many other features. In addition, the mobile app allows for a variety of other services, including, in some cases, telehealth.

The ease with which the platform allows individuals to interact with their insurance plans is clearly one of the most attractive features of this modern interface between users and the payers of their health benefits.

COLLAPSE OF THE GIANTS

While the ultimate success or failure of Oscar Health as a payer along with its investor owners has yet to be written, a dramatic example of caution with PE can be found in the story of Envision, a physician staffing company.

Recall in Chapter 13 that Dr. Sam Monroe had to address the contract and relationship with the local, independent ED group that was staffing his emergency department. When Sam called his old friend Geoff, he learned a number of things that kept him focused on retaining the local ED group and may have even influenced his decision to offer the group the revenue cycle services at a discount compared to their outside billing agency.

Geoff also indicated that some of the national physician staffing companies had negotiated with insurers for higher professional payment rates that were ultimately passed on to patients in terms of co-pays and the like.

Not only did Sam want to avoid that impact on patients (whether from an outside hospitalist or ED agency), but he particularly wanted to somehow integrate the ED group into the hospital operations. Tying the local ED group into the billing/collection services, he believed, would help the alignment of the group and the hospital and make it easier to press for more efficient throughput.

Additionally, he thought that this type of integration into finances and operations would keep the group from selling itself to a company that Sam and the hospital would have little control over. At the time, Sam knew nothing about the eventual collapse of Envision.

Envision Healthcare

Envision Healthcare was founded in 1992 as Emergency Medical Services Corp., a physician practice management company (recall Chapter 6) focused on physician groups in the areas of ED initially, and eventually anesthesia and radiology, a common triad of hospital-based physician groups.[11] With the capital provided by several major private investors, Envision grew quickly and began to acquire and own hospital-based physician groups.

Envision's rapid growth attracted the attention of additional investors including CD&R, which bought Envision for $3.2 billion in 2011 and subsequently took Envision public via IPO in 2013.[11]

The proceeds of the IPO amounted to just short of a $1 billion and it was reported that about half of that money would be used to redeem the outstanding notes, $450 million in principal and $17.2 million of accrued and unpaid interest.[11]

One of the most intriguing parts of investment management is the use of borrowing to finance large deals ("debt financing"). Some of the borrowing is from private investors/banks and some is from public institutional lenders/banks. Regardless, at some point, the debt has to be re-paid.

Envision's activity as a public company was marked by aggressive acquisition and growth strategies, including its 2016 merger with AmSurg, a leading ambulatory surgery center management company, but also marked with failed attempts to merge with a competitor PPM/physician staffing agency known as TeamHealth, which was acquired by Blackstone in the same year, 2016.[11]

Things were a bit choppy after acquiring AmSurg, and in 2018, private equity firm KKR (one of the early investors in Envision and ongoing shareholder) made the bold decision to take Envision Healthcare private.[11] KKR acquired the company for a staggering $9.9 billion, including a resounding $7 billion in debt financing – one of the largest leveraged buyouts at the time.[11]

As Sam learned in his exploration of physician contracting, companies like Envision Healthcare had pursued exorbitantly high rates from insurers to contract for physician services. When payers refused to foot the entire bill, Envision would pass along any leftover service bills to the patients, a practice known as "balance billing."

If payers refused to accept Envision's contract terms, Envision simply went out of network with them, leading to "surprise bills" for unknowing patients who were going to their preferred ED for emergency care believing that the hospital and services were all in-network.

As a result of this practice by several ED physician companies, The No Surprises Act (NSA), passed in 2020 and in effect as of 2022, aimed to protect patients from surprise medical bills resulting from out-of-network care.[12] Under the Act, physician groups and payers would have to enter into arbitration to resolve their disputes over charges.

In particular, UnitedHealth Group, one of the countries' largest insurance companies who just so happens to have its own (competitor) physician staffing company, Sound Physicians, refused to cooperate with Envision and through arbitration and lawsuits forced downward pressure on Envision's tactics and effectively lowered its revenue.[11]

Combined with the impact of the COVID-19 pandemic on vastly lowered emergency services and rising interest rates, Envision and its shareholders found themselves struggling under the weight of its massive debt burden.

Rating agencies downgraded all of their bonds and notes to "junk" level, which means that although the yield is high, the value of the bond is low and at great risk of a default, meaning that bondholders will never be re-paid. Many investors lose significant money under that scenario.

Despite numerous efforts to restructure and improve its financial outlook, Envision filed for bankruptcy in 2023.[11] Fortunately for patients and hospitals, the U.S. Bankruptcy Court allowed a pathway for Envision to continue to provide physician care and to avoid significant disruptions in EDs across the United States.[11,13]

Having said that, Envision's reputation (not to mention its physicians' careers) is likely significantly damaged and any/all shareholders, including physicians themselves, have suffered significant financial losses. Sam's instinct to avoid outside staffing agencies like Envision for his ED spared him.

Silicon Valley Bank

There is one more cautionary financial tale for rising physician executives to consider as they move about their career paths, and that is the story of Silicon Valley Bank (SVB). Willie Sutton may not have been the brightest bank robber ever, but he is best remembered for his famous line when asked in 1933 why he robbed all of the banks, "Because that's where the money is."

SVB was established in 1983 in San Jose, California, with a focus on supporting and lending to startup companies, particularly in the greater Silicon Valley area.[14]

The bank structured its loans with the understanding that startups do not earn revenue immediately, but that it could set up arrangements to collect deposits from those same startups that were financed through venture capital. As those startups matured, SVB would continue to create services to retain those businesses.

For example, initially, startup founders seeking loans from the bank had to pledge about half of their shares as collateral, which could be returned to the founders as loans were repaid. Whether or not the loans were paid back from elsewhere-borrowed capital or from general business revenue was of little concern. The bank, in turn, could sell those same startup shares to willing investors to cover startup failures or company losses.

SVB formally entered the private banking business in 2002 and by 2015, stated that it served 65% of all U.S. startups.[15] By the end of 2022, 56% of its loan portfolio were loans to VC and PE firms and about one-quarter of those loans in turn were to technology and healthcare companies, including startup companies.[15]

It became even more incestuous, as it then appeared that SVB and the venture capital firms seeking to put equity into a startup required the startups to conduct their banking at SVB.[15] Nothing seemed to prohibit the VC firms from setting up these arrangements.

SVB became the darling bank for many healthcare startups and was used by three-fourths of venture capital-back initial public offerings in healthcare since 2020, according to data once cited on its website.

It would appear to a novice, then, that most healthcare startups were receiving borrowed money from VC firms that were themselves borrowing from SVB and, in turn, the startups placed their discretionary cash, holdings, and/or revenue with the bank for safekeeping.

To the average person it appears exceedingly difficult to follow where the money trail started and where it ended. One of the companies that benefitted from this access to capital was Privia Health, a company that had $100 million in commitments to SVB.[16]

As 2022 was drawing to a close, economic conditions from the COVID-19 pandemic began to affect the access to venture capital. As the venture capital started drying up, many bank customers, including healthcare tech startup companies, withdrew their deposited money. SVB did not have the cash on hand to return those deposits, because all of that money was tied up in long-term investments, particularly bonds.

Remember how Sophie's colleagues teased her about her new skill related to LIBOR talks with banks? Banks deposit the money they receive in a variety of instruments (bonds/stocks/loan packages/ etc.) to safely harbor it and also to yield returns on the large sums of money. If Willie Sutton were alive in 2022, for him to steal the real value of SVB, he would first have to find where the money was tied up and be able to find buyers for the different instruments.

So, as businesses of all kinds withdrew from SVB, the bank started selling their bonds at a significant loss, which caused distress to customers and investors. Word got out quickly that SVB was selling large numbers of bonds and attempting to raise more than $1 billion in cash to meet the demands of its customers.

In one of the most astonishing events in U.S. banking history, particularly because so many of the key investors were connected via mobile devices and social media, SVB experienced a "run on the bank" as everyone suddenly wanted to withdraw their money. Companies needed cash to run their own operations and could not count on the bank to remain solvent.

SVB collapsed under the weight of the lightning fast run and within 48 hours of the first public report of the attempt to raise cash, on Friday, March 10, the bank was shut down by the state of California, seized by U.S. regulators, and placed under the control of the FDIC.[15]

Later that Friday night, while individuals and big companies anxiously awaited Monday morning and any pending announcements, Hemant Taneja, the CEO of the VC firm General Catalyst, who led the effort to organize support for SVB apparently over the effects of SVB on their industry, tweeted a statement of support for the bank, alongside 12 other PE/VC firms.[17]

Ultimately, about two weeks later, First Citizens Bank acquired SVB in a deal convened by U.S. regulators and the bank remains open for commercial banking.[15]

The full impact of the collapse is not yet known, but it is reasonable to assume several things: Investors in SVB lost money, PE/VC firms did not have the same level of success of obtaining loans from SVB due to restrictions, the flow of PE/VC money headed to healthcare startups would have dried up, and healthcare startups would have had to reduce operations and scale back growth to manage expenses against revenue.

While Oscar Health was quick to publicly announce that it had no deposits with SVB, Privia Health undoubtedly had to adjust its immediate financial operations until it could obtain access to its deposits.

The failure of SVB was the largest of any bank by assets (over $200 billion) since that time and caused fear in the finance world that the U.S. would quickly see a repeat of the "Great Recession of 2007-2008."

So, what does all of this have to do with the two things that stay with physicians their entire career? What does private equity want from healthcare startups? Why would Taneja want to show public support for SVB?

In the next chapter, we see how the future of healthcare remains tethered to the role of money and whether or not who takes call and how the money is split may have new meanings.

LESSONS LEARNED

- Whether or not they have an advanced degree in business or finance, a CMO must periodically check in with the CFO to better understand the economic backbone of the organization.
- The funding sources of the enterprise require due consideration. The sources may have particular agendas.
- For a CMO to continue to bring value and to drive quality and safety, they must be able to hold both in some regard at the same time. Some organizations may not put equal weight on both at the same time, which puts tension on the clinical leadership.
- Some healthcare business models are developed specifically to bring returns on investment and/or increase profitability rather than deliver patient-facing outcomes. The narrative of the latter may be useful messaging, but it may not be the underlying goal. Make sure you can align yourself with the organizational goals and objectives.
- Read business newspapers and internet sites. Sometimes disparate business stories intersect with the healthcare arena in ways that are not obvious at first glance.

QUESTIONS TO ASK

- Can PE/VC support the mission, vision, values of healthcare organizations?
- Who are the real leaders of PE/VC investment? Can PE/VC-backed physician leaders be trusted to deliver quality care? Does the title "physician" matter at that level? How would you decide?
- What alternatives do you have if your organization is soliciting PE/VC for financial support? If your organization was beginning to be supported by private funding, would you remain loyal and try your best to avoid the pitfalls described in this chapter?
- Is PE/VC the future financial funding for healthcare's future, especially in areas of efficiency, productivity, analytics, and outcomes? Is it going to be necessary?
- Is PE/VC just taking more slices of the already shrinking pie? Or is it the way to enlarge the pie? At what cost and to whom?
- Will consolidation continue? When do you foresee it happening where you live/work? Is it avoidable?
- Can small to medium-sized healthcare organizations remain locally owned and locally controlled? What happens when they cannot?

CHAPTER 17

Healthtech/Digital Health

"There's always an Arquillian Battle Cruiser, or a
Corillian Death Ray, or an intergalactic plague that is
about to wipe out all life on this miserable little planet,
and the only way these people can get on with their
happy lives is that they DO NOT KNOW ABOUT IT!"

Kay (Played by Tommy Lee Jones), "Men in Black"

IN 2015, AT THE AGE OF 72, Arthur Staley retired to Naples, Florida,
to live out his last years in the sun and warmth along the Gulf of
Mexico. He survived an episode of COVID-19 and through the mir-
acle (at least to him) of FaceTime and other video applications, he
was able to remain in contact with his children and grandchildren
who still lived in the Akron area.

As his health went up and down as a result of the infection that
damaged his lung and put him into Afib, he required two minor
hospitalizations, both done at home through a novel program
supported by CMS reimbursement known literally as hospital
at home.

He also benefited from remote monitoring to keep a close watch
on his heart rhythm that miraculously returned to a normal sinus
rhythm after his other systems gradually improved. This type of
monitoring would be crucial in the discussion with his cardiologist,
conducted via a telehealth visit, about how long to be medicated,
monitored, and the possibility of discontinuing his novel oral anti-
coagulant which required no regular monitoring, unlike the old days
when Dr. Staley prescribed warfarin.

Sophia Liontari was promoted from the regional chief medical
officer of the physician network company that she worked for to the
chief clinical officer (CCO) over the entire enterprise. She thrived in
the role until she became ill with Sjögren's syndrome with enough

symptoms of myofascial pain and fatigue that she decided to step away from the CCO role and take some time to reassess her career.

During her six months away from the hustle of a large thriving organization, she learned yoga and meditation, received the proper medical attention she had ignored for so long, believing her aches and fatigue were work-related, and found that she was feeling better overall. That's when she was approached to be an advisor for a healthcare startup.

The fledgling new company was founded by experienced individuals with well-established careers in healthcare who were all looking to fill in some gaps in the fragmented healthcare delivery system that they cut their teeth on.

The goal of the company was to establish a platform that coordinated elder care services and placed the patient in the center of the care management rather than inundating the patient with so many tasks and responsibilities that run counter to well-being in the first place. They wanted to make it easier for families (whether they lived near or far from the patient) as well as the immediate caregivers (spouse, private help) to support the care of the patient throughout their twilight years.

The care coordination would be supported by AI and would synthesize data, visits (both in-person and virtual), billing, medications, etc., so that being at the point of care was as friction-free as possible.

By this time, Sophie had come to terms that in order for these innovations to advance and to offer impactful solutions to patients and families, private equity would, at some point, be necessary to launch the platform. No other force was at work to drive these solutions to healthcare's most vexing and complicated problems, ones that evolved in the first place because of the fragmented system.

Sam Monroe had moved up the career ladder and served for a few years as the COO of Akron City Health, the parent company of the hospital, medical group, and health plan. He oversaw the coordinated response to the COVID-19 pandemic.

He engineered an increase in negative pressure/reverse isolation rooms, an increase in overall bed capacity, the accelerated use of telemedicine for both inpatient and outpatient care, alternative sites of care for surgical services, a massive community-based vaccine clinic, and myriad other significant requirements for the once-in-a-century calamity.

In the summer of 2023, when the system CEO retired, Sam was elevated to the role. In his wildest imagination, Sam never conceived of becoming the CEO of an integrated delivery network, much less becoming the first physician executive to serve in such a role and to be responsible for so many lives in the greater Akron area.

The community leaders welcomed Sam with open arms for multiple reasons, not the least of which was a desire by many of them that Sam would influence the forces of change that were intercepting the delivery of healthcare to the region.

Many of them were facing a wide range of economic and developmental issues and wanted reassurance that Sam would place individual health as his top priority. They had become pessimistic about the profiteering occurring in healthcare and the cost of health insurance, along with the cost of medications and other services required for healthy living. They wanted a doctor in charge who put their health and well-being above profit. At least that is what they wanted to believe.

The problem for Sam Monroe (and perhaps for Sophie Liontari and Art Staley as well) was that as fast as things were unfolding for them personally and professionally, the entire architecture of U.S. healthcare was undergoing ever more change and at an astonishing rate. In fact, by the time you have finished reading this book, so many things will have happened that a second edition with additional chapters might be required within short order.

EMERGING MODELS

The concept of vertical integration will be a key structure for healthcare delivery in the coming years, but in ways yet to be fully realized. While healthcare systems have created a variety of strategic partnerships and integrated networks to control the flow of money from payer to provider and all points in between, it is this proverbial circling of the wagons that appears to be protecting the cash distribution, rather than a wraparound service with the patient in the center, not the physician.

We have seen the slow and steady drumbeat of these sorts of models for several decades, all in an effort to capture more revenue in a time of shrinking reimbursements or changes in reimbursements altogether (e.g., value-based payments). It seems to be that on the surface the integrations are all about closing gaps in care, but essentially are structured to reduce waste, inefficiency, and to boost productivity and, if designed well enough, will improve the health of individuals and communities.

There are a few shining examples of physician-centered health systems, such as Cleveland Clinic and Mayo Clinic, whose outcomes are great examples of highly regarded patient outcomes-driven delivery models, but these are rather few and far between. Most local and regional health systems are unable to create the same type of world-renowned care due to any number of reasons.

HATCo

One of the most innovative integration models that has emerged and as of this writing has yet to prove itself, is the convergence of private equity and hospital management in the form of a health assurance transformation corporation (i.e., HATCo). Remember the primary author of the statement in support of Silicon Valley Bank in early 2023, Hemant Tenaja, the CEO of General Catalyst? Well, Tenaja, together with Dr. Marc Harrison, former CEO of Intermountain Healthcare, founded HATCo...

"to operationalize the promise of health assurance, and to demonstrate the economic and human benefits that result from collaboration and responsible innovation. The HATCo platform is designed to combine the best leadership and capabilities in healthcare and tech to inform, support and drive transformation enablement while *addressing system fragmentation* (emphasis added) and improving access to — and quality of — care. In collaboration with health system and technology leaders through partnerships, investments, and acquisitions, HATCo seeks to drive efficiency, affordability, and transparency to transform the healthcare industry to be more proactive, resilient, and equitable for communities and society."[1]

Further, a statement found on General Catalyst' website declares,

"HATCo's charter is not to disrupt healthcare systems; rather, it is to be in service of healthcare organizations everywhere to change how they deliver a *fundamentally better experience for consumers* (emphasis added) — and to prove the transformative effect of a true partnership between technologists, caregivers and capital. It is our belief that by making these organizations more profitable, more vibrant and more innovative, they will be better equipped to serve everyone in their communities with greater impact."[2]

General Catalyst is unabashedly framing their investment in HATCo as capital that is designed to generate profit in service to customers. The statement above says nothing about health outcomes, only about a better experience through transformation.

Along with that same declaration, dated October 8, 2023, the company outlined three ways in which they will accomplish their goal: HATCo will be working toward transformation with "20+ health system partners…to catalyze the health assurance ecosystem," "building an interoperability model" with the healthtech companies (in their portfolio), and "acquiring and operating a health system" in order to demonstrate their vision for transformation.[2]

In other words, a PE/VC incubator of healthtech will seek to run an entire health system containing those fledgling companies with a grand design of a novel digital health macro-ecosystem. This effort will not be without limitations and obstacles, but it is also nothing short of visionary at a minimum.

It also suggests that PE money continues to flow into healthcare at an extraordinary volume and rate. And true to their projections, in January 2024, HATCo announced a letter of intent to acquire Summa Health, "one of the largest integrated healthcare delivery systems in Ohio, encompassing a network of hospitals, community medical centers, a health plan, an accountable care organization, a multi-specialty physician organization, medical education, research and the Summa Health Foundation."[1]

According to Axios reporting, this is not expected to be a typical VC approach where investors seek the exit strategy from the onset in order to seek their return on the investment.[3] So, if private investors are seeking to place substantial amounts of time, money, resources, and their companies into healthcare, with HATCo seemingly the largest move into this space yet, what does this mean to the average CMO?

Other Major Movers

To answer this question, we need to look at a few more major movers in modern U.S. healthcare. The largest healthcare company by revenue, UnitedHealth Group Incorporated, mostly known for its commercial insurance portfolio founded in 1974 in Minnetonka, Minnesota, also operates Optum since 2011.

Optum, Inc., has several core capabilities, but most notably the company focuses on data and analytics, pharmacy care services, and physician employment.[4] According to Medscape in December 2023, UnitedHealth Group/Optum employs, contracts, or aligns with roughly 90,000 physicians in the country, which is about 1 in 10 practicing physicians in the U.S.[5] Furthermore, Optum has stated its revenue has surpassed $100 billion and contributes more than 50% of UnitedHealth's 2020 earnings.[6,7]

Not to be outdone, CVS has acquired Aetna, Walgreen's has acquired VillageMD, and Amazon now offers a subscription service for healthcare through its relationship with One Medical. These companies regularly interact with hundreds of millions of Americans and there is no escaping the impact that they will have on average persons in the coming years.

All these consolidated entities will leverage technology, data (purchase/spending/pharmaceutical usage, health habits), and customer base to drive more dollars through their portfolios.

While the majority of these are publicly traded companies, the interests of shareholders, particularly large investment fund managers, pension fund managers, and hedge fund managers, play significant roles in influencing the businesses in terms of returning profits to shareholders.

WHAT THIS MEANS FOR CMOs

With U.S. healthcare estimated as a $4 trillion industry, "there's gold in them thar hills," as Mark Twain wrote in his 1892 novel *The American Claimant*. Most individuals are unaware of the tremendous amount of money flowing in and out of the system, and understandably so, as when someone is ill, they are rarely seeking answers with Wall Street on their mind.

Which brings us back to the question: What do all of these consolidating moves mean for the average CMO?

Part of the answer depends in which care environment you find yourself. A hospital CMO will see a continued shift in care toward the sickest, most chronically ill patients on the admissions reports. Due to a multitude of factors, including ease and convenience, but mostly the current reimbursements against expenses, elective surgeries and procedures will migrate to ambulatory centers, as will many surgical and procedural specialists, making it harder to maintain call coverage, at least without adequate compensation to motivate someone to take hospital-based call.

A variety of profitable interventions will migrate away from the hospital and will create additional dynamic challenges for hospital operations and solvency.

For CMOs, these upheavals will impact patient care, as the OR teams may also migrate away and there will be the potential for a degradation of volume and experience in the ORs, both of which play a significant role in outcomes.

CMOs will have to work closely with the hospital leadership to consider ways to joint venture and rotate staff, if possible, between inpatient and outpatient sites. CMOs will have to consider what types of resources and tools are required to care for the ever-increasing high acuity patient population, learn how to design handoffs and care management to reduce unwanted/unnecessary re-admissions, and how to communicate with disparate primary care providers who may be disconnected from the hospital ecosystems.

What if the PCP works at Walgreens-OneMedical? Or lives within the cyberworld of Amazon? How is the information communicated and with what operating system? Who owns those systems and at whose costs?

Perhaps this is the vision of HATCo, an insular digital health system with amazing interoperability that provides a "closed system" of care from beginning to end. No worries about gaps in information, care plans, discharge instructions, etc.

Maybe the patient will ultimately be the center of all activity related to their recent illness and they will be blind to all of the systems that now "talk to each other." Maybe the types of things that irritated patients regarding their care will dissipate and they will tend to provide better ratings on all of the HCAHPs domains almost imperceptibly rather than by intention or design.

If you are the CMO of a large medical group, or involved in a system of large networks of providers, but not part of one of the more nationally based entities such as Optum, are you able to compete effectively with UnitedHealth for your preferred contract payment rates? If Optum practices are in proximity to your clinic, will you struggle to capture the UnitedHealth member market? Will Amazon take all of the bread and butter services away from your PCPs, such as sore throats, sinus congestion, backache, and stomachache?

Many of these conditions resolve with the tincture of time or with simple measures regardless of the practitioner, but if those visits with an Amazon provider are simple, convenient, perhaps even asynchronous, and result in a good outcome for the patient, what is the likelihood of them returning to your clinic that still operates with a physician-facing schedule and difficult access compared to digital doors elsewhere?

Will the clinic evolve into a place where only the sickest and most vulnerable turn for chronic care management, each patient with a list of issues much longer and more time consuming than an uncomplicated sore throat?

What if folks on MA plans are given home BP monitoring devices, blood glucose monitoring, and asynchronous remote telehealth options to optimize their conditions? How likely will they be to come to your clinic for a visit two or three times a year when the event is literally just a snapshot in time and does little to chronically manage a lifelong issue like diabetes?

System executives spend a great deal of time in boardrooms working through the "conditions of battlefield" as it is known. A CEO once shared with me that what got him up and out of bed every morning was the thrill of going off (in his Porsche) to work to slay dragons each day, never knowing what color dragon he would face or whether an invincible dragon had arrived at the castle gates and it would be his last day as CEO.

These are genuine issues for executives who manage large companies but are just as real in small and medium-sized markets of healthcare delivery. With bigger and bigger conglomerate forces lining up around the castle walls, the options become trickier by the day, and this was before the recent pandemic ignited labor shortages, supply chain interruptions, and higher acuity than ever because of delayed care.

For the foreseeable future, hospitals and clinics will be managing the ever-increasing dual complexities of internal needs and external forces with no obvious influx of new revenue or higher reimbursement; therefore, whether done locally or in partnership with others, systems will have to be innovative, nimble, creative, and, effective to withstand the volume of change with tight operating revenue or limited access to capital.

When the average physician complains to the CMO about how the OR closes at 3:00 in the afternoon and that his elective case cannot be re-scheduled for several days, the CMO must recognize that the surgeon likely has little knowledge about the forces that led to such a decision.

The CMO must be prepared to understand how the choice of managing the splitting of the hospital's money (and/or limited staff resources) affects the splitting of someone else's money and affects a patient.

A CMO cannot simply take the surgeon's complaint up to the executive boardroom and expect that the complaint will be heard, much less tolerated. The CMO needs to advocate for strategies that support a variety of stakeholders, but most importantly the patient.

LESSONS LEARNED

- Private equity seeks to help companies mature and/or to enable a path for growth for an expected return on investment.
- Venture capital is a form of private equity and seeks to launch startups with the goal of an exit from the startup.
- VC firms can see their investments returned upon exit, by the takeover of PE. Sometimes, these two money management groups are actually part of the same entity and work for each other's benefit.
- Hospitals traditionally acquired capital from bonds, taxation, stocks, etc., along with the ability to "pay" for things from their operating income. Today, those opportunities are not as accessible, hence some of the infusion of PE/VC.
- PE/VC sees the vastness of the fragmented healthcare system and sees opportunity to invest in companies that can profit in that environment. It remains to be seen if they are becoming middleman between payers and providers or if there are other areas of cash flow that they seek to siphon.
- Vertical integration can occur within health systems or can be engineered by outside entities (sometimes fueled by PE/VC, but also by publicly traded companies, or both) that impact a non-integrated system.
- There are lateral and horizontal structures of integration, depending on whether there is a specific product (e.g., pharmaceutical) to be delivered or a service (chronic care management) to be provided. Integration is important to the profitability of the enterprise.
- The disruptions in the healthcare system may be multifactorial. As our understanding of disease becomes more complex, along with the growing number of elderly with advanced conditions, along with the many varieties of interventions, the care of any single patient has created a vast network of requirements that never before existed.

- Individual companies are seeking to engage in the fragmented components of healthcare delivery with new tools and technologies.
- Money is flooding both the fragments of care and the digital/tech companies seeking to prosper from those opportunities.
- The law of unintended consequences will play an outsized role in systems that are too late in recognizing how the new entries are going to disrupt their core services. Progressive companies with available capital will be able to shift where patients receive care and, ultimately, who is unable to do so. The diversion of patients will divert revenue. One system's gain is another's loss.

QUESTIONS TO ASK

- Who/what are the players in your environment that might or intentionally seek to disrupt the type of care your system delivers?
- Can you model out responses to changes in your local environment that protect the quality and safety of the care you seek to deliver?
- If your system seeks a strategic partner, do you have the information you need to determine the potential partner's reputation for patient care? What recommendations are you empowered to make to the CEO of your facility, institution, organization, system?
- What would you do if approached to be acquired by a PE/VC company? What is your role?
- What would you do if a Summa-like full wraparound digital health ecosystem proved to be successful? What if a HATCo-like company sought to sell you products that were developed while overseeing a full digital health ecosystem? What parameters would be important: patient experience, growth of services, health outcomes, process measures, value-based income enhancement? Who would be involved in those decisions?
- Can you distinguish between profit and greed? What about profiteering and greediness? When does the pursuit of profit

have negative consequences on patient care? Are there examples of positive consequences of profit in healthcare?
- Is the U.S. government moving more and more of CMS' expenditures into the hands of private industry (e.g., Medicare Advantage)? Should it or shouldn't it?
- Why do we call it value-based care? Value for whom: the payer or the patient?
- Why don't we call it (or lobby for) outcome-based care? Or fee for outcome? Is that even possible?

EPILOGUE

WHEN DR. BILL NADEAU RENDERED HIS OPINION to Dr. Puff Ballard, he spoke directly and honestly and told his old friend that he was diagnosing him with dementia. Out of professional courtesy, Bill waived his fee to his lifelong friend and longtime colleague. Bill gave Puff exactly what he needed: an answer to the problem with the choices in front of him.

The practice of medicine by its very nature seeks to understand, treat, and in some cases, eliminate disease. The practice is also by its very nature a business, an organized entity producing a service. It takes money to produce the service.

The modern state of healthcare should continue the noble and lifelong pursuit of caring for people in need and, regardless of how complex the condition or the myriad support structures in place to assist those in need and/or treat those conditions, the price to treat should not be the organizing principle by which care is delivered. Pricing and cost should be the engine that makes the healthcare train function and run on time, not the drivers leading to an unhealthy destination or system deterioration.

When Bill decided to waive the fee, he essentially disregarded every expense he had ever personally incurred (tuition, license fee, receptionist salary, paper clips, and even stamps) and subconsciously found that he couldn't focus on much else other than delivering the news to his dear old friend. On that particular day, he couldn't have determined what would be the appropriate fee even if he wanted to. Would the fee adequately pay for his knowledge, his diagnostic acumen, his examination skills, much less his empathy and soft (but firm) delivery of the diagnosis?

The practice of medicine remains a noble pursuit. At its core must be a love of humanity, and nickel and diming everyone is hurting more than helping. Physicians must lead the transformation of care with renewed attention to its delivery. New ideas are required to pair new values and payment models. Policymakers must re-evaluate the goal of the payment.

These are ostensibly auspicious goals. Chief medical officers are well positioned to re-consider ways of taking the necessary baby steps back to the humanity of medical practice. Perhaps some will consider a way to pay salaries to hospitalists based on time studies, how to collect and deliver lump sums to the entire physician team in charge of spinal care, how to negotiate for appropriate prepayments and skip all of the individual fees trapped in the revenue cycle processes that drain so much in terms of time, resources, and money.

Maybe CMOs of insurance companies will demand that contracted providers (physicians, hospitals, ASCs, clinics) will offer the same results and outcomes that are expected in peer review. Maybe CMOs can work together and agree on an approach to personalized care and then personalize the price of that care, too.

If only a certain percentage of patients will experience blood loss/transfusion with a cardiac catheterization, then guarantee that percentage to the payer and give back the payer's money if/when the percentage goal is not met. In that case, agree to place the contract on a focused review and performance plan (analogous to an OPPE/FPPE) until you have corrected for the outlier events or simply re-negotiate what variability in blood loss is clinically acceptable and bake that expense into the new "global" payment for cardiac catheterizations. Maybe this idea will spread into new models of "fee-for-outcome" payments.

Prepay for specific outcomes when attempting to generate capitation arrangements, rather than expecting certain indirect, if not burdensome, processes and performance measures to be created.

Try to find risk sharing or alternative ways to pay for the direct and immediate beneficial impact on patient care. In parallel, find systems and processes that enable the physician to have more time to deliver the right care and then ask the payers to pay for that infrastructure.

The result is better health outcomes, contrary to systems that are more efficient with their physician time and see insurers simply ending up paying more for increased productivity now that the physicians have more time to see more patients.

Leaders must find ways to align the incentives that are miserably mis-aligned today. Guarantee that every beneficiary of some type of health coverage can have more time and better results with physicians in the office, in the clinic, in the ED, in the OR, and at the bedside. Is it possible to incentivize time? To incentivize outcome? To incentivize the clinical expertise of the team? These are questions that must be addressed if anything is to change.

Decide if you prefer the payer side, the provider side, acute care, long-term care, rehab care, Healthtech, or something else altogether. Decide if you prefer the challenges of population health, reducing inequities and bias, insurance companies, telemedicine, retail medicine, rural locations, critical care, highly specialized care, FQHCs, or something not yet even developed.

Regardless of those preferences and decisions, when you make your leap to become a physician executive and as you advance your career, take a hard look at the future through a new lens. Does the proposal in front of you split up the money? Shuffle the money? Pass the money through to another destination? Can the money stop being split altogether? Can healthcare even function without splitting up the money all of the time? And what can you possibly do about it?

The Future of Medicine

"You go to war with the army you have, not the army
you might want or wish to have at a later time."

Donald Rumsfeld

DONALD RUMSFELD, AN ILLINOIS-BORN Eagle Scout, naval aviator, Congressman, and two-time Secretary of Defense, earned recognition as the Outstanding Chief Executive Officer in the Pharmaceutical Industry in 1980 as the CEO of G.D. Searle & Company, a worldwide pharmaceutical company based in Skokie, Illinois. He was known, among many things (both praiseworthy and highly controversial) for many interesting quips and quotes.

Rumsfeld clearly was a pragmatist, if not a stoic, by espousing that you must do the best you can, with what you have, no matter where you are. And, yet categorically he was always thinking ahead. Whether about plans, tactics, optics, politics, or just day to day things, he kept an eye on the future of things to protect his president, his boss.

One of the most important things that a CMO can do is bring value to their boss as well as to the organization. This value can come in many forms.

TRENDS IN HEALTHCARE

Given what you have read and absorbed over these many pages, I believe it would be instructive to leave you with a sense of what some thought leaders are saying about the future of healthcare, what is unfolding as far as the healthcare environment, and how to position oneself among the expected trends.

Retail Health

The single most easily identified trend in recent years is the concept of retail health. As briefly mentioned in the prior chapter, every major retailer is leaning into the delivery of services and products in the world of healthcare.

Some have flopped and some have succeeded, but given enough time and money, one can expect some real winners to emerge. It would be wise to consider at least the possibilities, anyway.

As mentioned, Amazon will offer a subscription-based service for basic, non-complicated health needs ranging from telehealth visits to next-day medication delivery (or maybe even same day!), all for a single low, annual price just like Amazon Prime.

This is likely to be attractive to millions of young people who have few health needs and low discretionary income, for whom health insurance whether employed or not is simply unaffordable.

Dollar Stores, Inc., one of the largest retailers in rural areas with over 18,000 stores, is piloting several initiatives to provide point-of-care services with either telemedicine approaches or direct, onsite advance practice practitioners.

Centers for Excellence

Walmart, experimenting with a variety of onsite clinic models for its customer shopping base, has already influenced the healthcare industry by contracting (through its employer-sponsored health plans) with Centers of Excellence (COE).

The most well-known of these are centered around cardiac care and low back pain, two of the most common conditions of employees working for any large employer.

Employees on these plans who suffer these conditions are essentially directed to world-class care locations, not just because of the chosen health system's reputation in healthcare, but because they proved to Walmart that they could deliver world-class care at a lower price!

This keeps the medical expenses of the health plan (remember the MLR?) stable and, therefore, keeps the premiums from rising and the direct costs for the employee from rising, while returning them to work in satisfactory health.

This is a major return on investment for Walmart by keeping an eye on the cost of its share of the employer-sponsored healthcare benefit and by keeping a productive and engaged (if not grateful) workforce in place.

The COEs that serve Walmart patients are exceptionally well-positioned to enlarge their capacity and reap all of the potential benefits of value-based care from a variety of payer sources.

With a proven track record, any COE that has established bona fides and outcomes based results will be in a very strong position to negotiate for premium value-based payments, ones markedly better perhaps, than those granted to other providers.

Direct Primary Care

Perhaps the most striking form of what might be categorized as another form of retail health is the direct primary care (DPC) model, a trend that harkens back to Dr. Henry Ballard.

In DPC, primary care physicians forgo all insurance and third-party payments and offer their services for a monthly or an annual fee. Similar to Amazon's subscription price, the PCP asks for a flat payment and in return serves as the patient's primary care physician.

This model frees up the PCP from all of the hassles of accepting third-party payments. No longer does the office have to have multiple software products for billing/claims/adjudication/collection. No longer does the office have to worry about being dropped from a health plan or having payments reduced. No longer do the physician and staff have to manage prior authorizations, peer-to-peer reviews, and other barriers to offering the care plan to the patient.

As of this writing, with about half of all practicing physicians identifying as PCPs, about 4–5% of those doctors utilize this model. And while the typical number of patients in a panel is about half of the average employed physician, the trend of PCPs entering into DPC is slowly growing.

The physicians appear to be more satisfied with their practice regarding pace, stress, and income. Undoubtedly for common issues and as a gateway to referrals and other more labor-intensive care, patients seem to be quite receptive to this type of care model.

Finally, there are reasons to believe that federal administrators may encourage the model by allowing for individuals to use their health savings account dollars to pay for DPC and possibly CMS will create a payment model/subscription fee for its beneficiaries who seek the model.

How far this penetrates the healthcare market is yet to be seen, and how patients navigate complex care needs if/when they arise under these models is also not fully known, but it is a significant trend to monitor.

INSURER STRATEGIES

Lastly, it does appear that while the large insurers such as United, Blue Cross, Cigna, and Aetna continue to integrate across various elements of the macro healthcare system to control costs, they may be entering into more and more arrangements that finally recognize that value and outcomes demand more attention.

Insurers continue to work with large provider networks on capitations, bundled payments, performance payments, and the like with more risk sharing (so called "two-sided" risk model) between payer and provider.

HATCo, for example, will be well-poised to experiment within its new digital health ecosystem to monitor and manage health and outcomes of its patients through data analytics and interoperable health information/EHRs from the outpatient, to inpatient, and possibly post-acute care, and back again.

With continuous monitoring and management, perhaps HATCo will find a way to produce not just better patient experience (and not just more members signing up to pay premiums) but better outcomes.

Imagine a system that not only stops taking smaller and smaller pieces of the proverbial pie, but one that grows a bigger and bigger (more insured patients) pie that looks and tastes better each time you take a piece (e.g., better outcomes for more people).

ACCOUNTABLE CARE ORGANIZATIONS

In parallel, whether by coincidence or design I cannot say, CMS has stated that they envision every Medicare beneficiary to be enrolled in some sort of accountable care organization by 2030. Currently half of all seniors are on Medicare Advantage plans, which will serve as a way for the private sector to manage and coordinate their benefits and care and can do so in concert with the structure of ACOs. With so many individuals in these value-based arrangements, provider organizations will have to bend toward offering services that produce the desired outcomes and to accept the risk sharing that will be involved in the payment models.

The efforts of CMS to move to alternative payment models have been in effect for a solid decade, if not longer, and there is no initiative on the horizon to change this. While largely directed at population health strategies and primary care, there have also been models for specialty care.

For example, orthopedics has been on the leading edge with years of bundled payments (e.g., BPCI) and given that so much of the care is episodic (e.g., TKA or THA), this may or may not result in transferable payment models for other specialties and is yet to be fully known.

What is also still unclear is how the various specialists who function in an FFS model will be asked to adapt to new payments or if ultimately those physicians will be left alone in FFS, with a largely hybridized payment structure across the different sites of service.

ALL THINGS TO EVERYONE?

Regardless, with so many forces in play from so many directions, generic systems need to consider and frequently re-consider what their primary focus will be, on what patients, and with what conditions. Other newly emerging systems, like HATCo and Summa, may be able to be all things to all payers and to all patients, but that will have to play itself out.

If we are somehow lucky, each of these care models will bend back toward the patient and deliver a full wraparound service like the old days of Dr. Ballard when the primary relationship was between the doctor and the patient and everything else just seemed to work itself out.

The dominant trends of integration, consolidation, population health, retail health, and value-based care converging onto operational DPCs, ACOs, and COEs will influence how healthcare is delivered at a macro level for the near future. Whether or not public policy (e.g., pharmaceutical price controls, limits on prior authorizations) or new paradigms (e.g., healthcare as a public utility, especially in rural areas) unfold and alter the course of the current healthcare marketplace will depend on other forces that are beyond the frame of this primer.

And yet, in some ways, even at these leading indicator macro level changes there are still going to be two things that stay with physicians (including CMOs) throughout their careers. Physician leaders, not just the front-line doctors, will have to continuously ask themselves as the future unfolds: Who is splitting the money? Who should be splitting the money? And, at the end of the day, who is really responsible for the care of the patient?

AFTERWORD

THE HISTORY OF MEDICINE is very well documented, along with volumes of material on the finances of healthcare. This book is a part of that large body of carefully crafted tomes, many of which reveal more layers and nuances than we can explore in this one.

This book is the result of several things, but its origins date back to an almost random call from Nancy Collins, a seasoned publisher specializing in medicine and the business of medicine, now the senior vice president for content procurement at AAPL.

When I retired from being a chief medical officer, I decided to try my hand at writing and with my very first submission (to AAPL, of course), I received a phone call from Nancy asking to explore the piece with me. From there and after several more conversations, Nancy connected me with Dr. Mark Olszyk, who along with Dr. Rex Hoffman, was editing *The Chief Medical Officer's Essential Guidebook*.

With Nancy's support I was given an opportunity to join Mark, Rex, and many others and to write a chapter for the *Guidebook*. From that moment I knew that I had re-kindled a long since buried piece of my past: writing.

After the *Guidebook* was published, Nancy and I collaborated again and determined that there was a tremendous desire among novice physician leaders to read and to learn more about the world of the CMO. Together we drew up the idea to prepare a book that would focus on the business and finance of healthcare written specifically for the aspiring CMO audience.

By no means is this book exhaustive, but it should be instructive to those who have been so busy learning the language of medicine that they are essentially illiterate in this other language.

I am forever indebted to Nancy for picking up the phone that day. I owe even more to Mark, who has been an inspiration from the start, and without whom I would not have been lucky enough to have found myself involved in so many CMO-related activities.

I also want to extend my gratitude to Dr. Steven Brass and the rest of the original Chicago Six, including Dr. Reka Danko and Dr.

Elizabeth Warren. Steven has been both a *mensch* to me and a great sounding board for my thoughts.

Similarly, I must thank the many CMOs I have come to know during this effort. I have made many new friends and I have re-connected with several old ones. The CMO community is not that large and is one of the most untapped and priceless resources in modern healthcare right now.

There is one other small group that bears mentioning. This is a special group of guys that I have grown up with. They are the real pioneers of what it means to be a physician leader. Each one of them helped make me what I am today, each in their own unique way. A few of us still get together now and again to discuss a delightful book and to share a bottle (or two) of red wine even after nearly 30 years. We have been through more joy and pain than any band of brothers has a right to. Not sure if they remember, but I wore #144 on my jersey and I was damn proud to do so.

REFERENCES

Preface

1. Collins J. *Good to Great*. London. Random House. 2001: 72–97.
2. Hlavin J. CMO Experiences: A Rudimentary Case Report. *Physician Leadership Journal*. 2019; 6(5):43–49.
3. Olszyk M. *The Chief Medical Officer's Essential Guidebook*. Washington, DC. American Association for Physician Leadership; 2023: xxii.
4. Hertling M. *Growing Physician Leaders*. New York: Rosetta Brooks. 2016: 23.
5. Hertling M. Personal communication.

Chapter 1

1. Barnes J. Moving Away From Fee-for-Service. *The Atlantic*. May 7, 2012. https://www.theatlantic.com/health/archive/2012/05/moving-away-from -fee-for-service/256755/
2. Millenson M. Medicare, Fair Pay, and the AMA: The Forgotten History. *Health Affairs*. September 10, 2015. https://www.healthaffairs.org/content/ forefront/medicare-fair-pay-and-ama-forgotten-history
3. Arrow, KJ. Uncertainty and The Welfare Economics of Medical Care. *The American Economic Review*. 1963; 53:941–973.

Chapter 2

1. Carey, D. Nanticoke Hospital Toasts 100 Years. *Times-Leader*. July 18, 2009. https://www.timesleader.com/archive/1251845/nanticoke-hospital -toasts-100-years
2. Morrisey, M. *Health Insurance, Second Edition*. Chicago, IL. Health Administration Press. 2013:6.
3. Consumer Reports. Blue Cross and Blue Shield: A Historical Compilation. March 2013. https://advocacy.consumerreports.org/wp-content/uploads/ 2013/03/yourhealthdollar.org_blue-cross-history-compilation.pdf
4. Cunningham R, Cunningham RM. The Blues: History of the Blue Cross and Blue Shield System. Northern Illinois University Press. 1997.
5. Numbers R. The Third Party: Health Insurance in America. In *The Therapeutic Revolution: Essays in the History of Medicine*, ed. Vogal, HJ and Rosenberg, CE. Philadelphia: University of Pennsylvania Press. 1979: 177–200.
6. Schumann RE. Compensation from World War II through the Great Society. U.S. Bureau of Labor Statistics. January 30, 2003. https://www.bls.gov/opub/ mlr/cwc/compensation-from-world-war-ii-through-the-great-society.pdf
7. Morrisey M. *Health Insurance, Second Edition*. Chicago, IL. Health Administration Press. 2013:9.
8. Wikipedia. The Burton Act. https://en.wikipedia.org/wiki/Hill%E2% 80%93Burton_Act

Chapter 3

1. U.S. Health Insurance Industry Analysis Report: 2022 Results. National Association of Insurance Commissioners. https://content.naic.org/sites/default/files/inline-files/Health%202022%20Annual%20Industry%20Report.pdf
2. Insurance Handbook. Insurance Information Institute. 2010. https://www.iii.org/publications/insurance-handbook/regulatory-and-financial-environment/reinsurance
3. Fox PD, Kongstvedt PR, ed. A History of Managed Health Care and Health Insurance in the United States. *The Essentials of Managed Health Care*. 6th ed. Burlington, MA: Jones & Bartlett Learning; 2013:4.
4. Blue Cross and Blue Shield of Ohio. Encyclopedia of Cleveland History. Cleveland, OH: Case Western Reserve University. https://case.edu/ech/articles/b/blue-cross-blue-shield-ohio
5. USA Facts. https://usafacts.org/data/topics/people-society/population-and-demographics/population-data/population/
6. Wikipedia. Coronary Artery Bypass Surgery. https://en.wikipedia.org/wiki/Coronary_artery_bypass_surgery
7. Wikipedia. Medicare. https://en.wikipedia.org/wiki/Medicare_(United_States)#Payment_for_services
8. Fox PD, Kongstvedt PR, ed. A history of Managed Health Care and Health Insurance in the United States. *The Essentials of Managed Health Care*. 6th ed. Burlington, MA: Jones & Bartlett Learning; 2013:6.

Chapter 4

1. Wikipedia. Medicare. https://en.wikipedia.org/wiki/Medicare_(United_States)#Payment_for_services
2. Tseng P, Kaplan RS, Richman BD, *et al*. Administrative Costs Associated with Physician Billing and Insurance-Related Activities at an Academic Health Care System. *JAMA*. 2018;319(7):691–697.
3. Anderson GF, Reinhardt UE, Hussey PS, *et al*. It's the Prices, Stupid: Why the United States Is so Different From Other Countries. *Health Affairs*. 2003;22(3):89–105.
4. Morrisey, M. *Health Insurance, 2nd ed*. Chicago, IL: Health Administration Press. 2013:19.
5. Hirsch JA, Nicola G, McGinty G, *et al*. ICD-10: History and Context. *Am J Neuroradiol*. 2016;37(4):596–599.
6. Centers for Medicare and Medicaid Services. Design and Development of the Diagnosis Related Group (DRG). CMS website. https://www.cms.gov/icd10m/version37-fullcode-cms/fullcode_cms/Design_and_development_of_the_Diagnosis_Related_Group_(DRGs).pdf

Chapter 5

1. Morrisey M. *Health Insurance, 2nd ed*. Chicago, IL: Health Administration Press. 2013:19.

2. Guterman S, Dobson A. Impact of the Medicare Prospective Payment System for Hospitals. *Health Care Financ Rev*. 1986;7(3):97–114.

3. Congressional Budget Office. The Prices That Commercial Health Insurers and Medicare Pay for Hospitals' and Physicians' Services. U.S. Government. January 1, 2022. https://www.cbo.gov/system/files/2022-01/57422-medical-prices.pdf

4. Lopez E, Neuman T, Jacobson G, Levitt L. How Much More Than Medicare Do Private Insurers Pay? A Review of the Literature. KFF. April 15, 2020. https://www.kff.org/medicare/issue-brief/how-much-more-than-medicare-do-private-insurers-pay-a-review-of-the-literature/

5. Guterman S, Eggers PW, Riley G, Greene TF, Terrell SA. The First 3 Years of Medicare Prospective Payment: An Overview. *Health Care Financ Rev*. 1988;9(3):67–77.

6. Applied Policy, LLC. GPOs: Helping to Increase Efficiency and Reduce Costs for Healthcare Providers and Suppliers Applied Policy. October 2014. https://www.supplychainassociation.org/wp-content/uploads/2018/05/Applied_Policy_Report_2014.pdf

7. Wikipedia. https://en.wikipedia.org/w340BDrugPricingProgram.iki/340B_Drug_Pricing_Program

Chapter 6

1. Encyclopedia.com. PhyCor, Inc. https://www.encyclopedia.com/books/politics-and-business-magazines/phycor-inc

2. Sharpe A. PhyCor Finds Managing, Merging Physician Practices Is Difficult Task. *The Wall Street Journal*. May 4, 1998. https://www.wsj.com/articles/SB893991750857346500

Chapter 7

1. Royce TJ, Schenkel C, Kirkwood, K, *et. al.* Impact of Pharmacy Benefit Managers on Oncology Practices and Patients *JCO Oncology Practice*. 2020;16(5):276–284.

2. Parasrampuria S, Murphy S. Trends in Prescription Drug Spending, 2016-2021. Washington, DC: Office of the Assistant Secretary for Planning and Evaluation, U.S. Department of Health and Human Services. September 2022. https://aspe.hhs.gov/sites/default/files/documents/88c547c976e915fc31fe2c6903ac0bc9/sdp-trends-prescription-drug-spending.pdf

3. Elkind P. Vulgarians at the Gate How Ego, Greed, and Envy Turned MedPartners from a Hot Stock into a Wall Street Fiasco. CNN Money. June 21, 1999. https://money.cnn.com/magazines/fortune/fortune_archive/1999/06/21/261719/

4. Consumer Reports. Blue Cross and Blue Shield: A Historical Compilation. March 2013. https://advocacy.consumerreports.org/wp-content/uploads/2013/03/yourhealthdollar.org_blue-cross-history-compilation.pdf

5. Martin B. CareMark and MedPartners A HealthSouth Protégé. https://www.
bmartin.cc/dissent/documents/health/healthsouth_crmk_medpt.html

6. Barlett DL, Steele JB. *Critical Condition: How Health Care in America
Became Big Business & Bad Medicine.* New York, NY: Doubleday; 2004.

Chapter 8

1. Bailes JS, Coleman TS. The Long Battle Over Payment for Oncology Services
in the Office Setting. *JCO Oncology Practice.* 2014; 10(1):1–4.

2. American Medical Association. Development of the Resource-Based Relative
Value Scale. AMA. https://www.ama-assn.org/system/files/development-of-
the-resource-based-relative-value-scale.pdf

3. USC-Brookings Schaeffer Initiative for Health Policy. The Medicare
Physician Fee Schedule Likely To Serve as Foundation for Alternative
Payment Models. 2017. https://www.brookings.edu/wp-content/
uploads/2017/08/medicare-pfs-conference-brief-event-summary.pdf

4. Baadh A, Peterkin Y, Wegener M, *et. al.* The Relative Value Unit: History,
Current Use, and Controversies. *Current Problems in Diagnostic Radiology.*
2016;45(2):128–132.

5. Kolber M. Stark Regulation: A Historical and Current Review of the Self-
Referral Laws. *HEC Forum.* 2006;18(1):61–84.

Chapter 9

1. Kaiser Family Foundation. Timeline: History of Health Reform in the U.S.
KFF.org. https://www.kff.org/wp-content/uploads/2011/03/5-02-13-history-
of-health-reform.pdf

2. Sprague L. Meaningful Use of Health Information Technology: Proving Its
Worth? *National Health Policy Forum Brief* (No. 856). Washington, DC:
George Washington University Press. November 2015.

3. Gladwell M. *The Tipping Point: How Little Things Can Make a Big
Difference.* New York: Back Bay Books. 2002:291–293.

4. Centers for Medicare and Medicaid Services. Medicare & Medicaid
EHR Incentive Program. CMS website. 2010. https://www.cms.gov/
Regulations-and-Guidance/Legislation/EHRIncentivePrograms/downloads/
mu_stage1_reqoverview.pdf

5. Sinsky C, Colligan L, Li L, *et. al.* Allocation of Physician Time in Ambulatory
Practice: A Time and Motion Study in 4 Specialties. *Annals of Internal
Medicine.* 2016;165:753–760.

6. Gold M, McLaughlin C. Assessing HITECH Implementation and Lessons: 5
Years Later. *Milbank Q.* 2016;94(3):654–687.

7. American Medical Association. AMA/Specialty Society RVS Update
Committee Summary of Recommendations. April 2019. https://www.ama-
assn.org/system/files/2020-11/may-2019-ruc-recommendations-office-visits.
pdf

8. GE HealthCare. GE Medical Systems Completes Acquisition of MedicaLogic Business to Expand Electronic Medical Record Offering. Press Release. GE HealthCare. March 26, 2002. https://www.gehealthcare.com/about/newsroom/press-releases/ge-medical-systems-completes-acquisition-medicalogic-business-expand-electronic?npclid=botnpclid#:~:text=GE%20Medical%20Systems%20Information%20Technologies,for%20%2435.25%20million%20in%20cash

9. GE HealthCare. GE to Acquire Millbrook to Create Digital Doctor's Office of the Future. Press Release. GE HealthCare. November 2002. https://www.gehealthcare.com/about/newsroom/press-releases/ge-acquire-millbrook-create-digital-doctors-office-future

10. GE HealthCare. GE Healthcare to Acquire IDX Systems Corporation; Significantly Expands GE Presence in Healthcare Information Technologies. Press Release. GE HealthCare. September 2005. https://www.gehealthcare.com/middle-east/about/newsroom/press-releases/ge-healthcare-acquire-idx-systems-corporation-significantly-expands-ge-presence#:~:text=GE%20Healthcare%20will%20help%20accelerate,core%20of%20our%20IT%20systems.

11. Miliard M. Athenahealth's Centricity Business is now athenaIDX. Healthcare IT News. July 15, 2020. https://www.healthcareitnews.com/news/athenahealths-centricity-business-now-athenaidx

Chapter 10

1. Kaiser Family Foundation. Timeline: History of Health Reform in the U.S. KFF. May 2013. https://www.kff.org/wp-content/uploads/2011/03/5-02-13-history-of-health-reform.pdf

2. Centers for Medicare and Medicaid Services. What Are the Value-Based Programs? CMS website. https://www.cms.gov/medicare/quality/value-based-programs

3. The National Academies. Accounting for Social Risk Factors in Medicare Payment: Identifying Social Risk Factors. Washington, DC: National Academies Press; 2016. https://nap.nationalacademies.org/read/21858/chapter/3

4. Watson I. The Utilization Review Process and the Origins of Medical Necessity. Blog. MCG.com. June 21, 2018. https://www.mcg.com/blog/2018/06/21/utilization-review-medical-necessity/

5. Wolters Kluwer. Expert Insights. HCAHPS Scores: History, Goals, and Impacts. Blog. Wolters Kluwer. November 30, 2018. https://www.wolterskluwer.com/en/expert-insights/hcahps-scores-history-goals-and-impacts

6. Centers for Medicare and Medicaid Services. Fact Sheet: First Release of the Overall Hospital Quality Star Rating on Hospital Compare. CMS website. June 27, 2016. https://www.cms.gov/newsroom/fact-sheets/first-release-overall-hospital-quality-star-rating-hospital-compare

7. Yakusheva O, Hoffman GJ. Does a Reduction in Readmissions Result in Net Savings for Most Hospitals? An Examination of Medicare's Hospital Readmissions Reduction Program. *Med Care Res Rev*. 2020;77(4):334–344.
8. Centers for Medicare and Medicaid Services. Overall Hospital Quality Star Rating. CMS website. https://data.cms.gov/provider-data/topics/hospitals/overall-hospital-quality-star-rating

Chapter 11

1. Ryan C. Explaining the Medicare Sustainable Growth Rate. American Action Forum Insight. March 26, 2015. http://americanactionforum.aaf.rededge.com/uploads/files/insights/2015-03-25_Explaining_the_Medicare_Sustainable_Growth_Rate.pdf
2. Centers for Medicare and Medicaid Services. Quality Payment Program. CMS website. https://qpp.cms.gov/
3. Kocot SL, White R, Tu T, Muhlestein D. The Impact of Accountable Care: Origins and Future of Accountable Care Organizations. Brookings Research. May 12, 2015. https://www.brookings.edu/wp-content/uploads/2016/06/impact-of-accountable-careorigins-052015.pdf
4. Landi H. Physician Enablement Company Privia Health Pops In Public Debut With Outsized IPO. Fierce Healthcare. May 2, 2021. https://www.fiercehealthcare.com/tech/physician-enablement-company-privia-health-pops-public-debut-outsized-ipo
5. Borchert R. Privia Health Reports Results in CMS' Medicare Shared Savings Program for the 2022 Performance Year. Press Release. Privia Health. August 25, 2023. https://www.priviahealth.com/press-release/privia-health-reports-results-in-cms-medicare-shared-savings-program-for-the-2022-performance-year/
6. Gatlin A. Privia Health Says It's The Uber Of Managed Care — Here's What That Means. Investor's Business Daily. July 1, 2022. https://www.investors.com/research/the-new-america/prva-stock-how-this-bullish-ipo-is-enabling-doctors-to-succeed/

Chapter 14

1. Harrington S. Medical Loss Ratio Regulation under the Affordable Care Act. *Inquiry Journal*. 2013;50:9–26.
2. Ortaliza J, Amin K, Cox C. KFF: 2023 Medical Loss Ratio Rebates. KFF website. May 17, 2023. https://www.kff.org/private-insurance/issue-brief/medical-loss-ratio-rebates/
3. Livingston S. The Medical Loss Ratio's Mixed Record. *Modern Healthcare*. March 14, 2020. https://www.modernhealthcare.com/insurance/medical-loss-ratios-mixed-record
4. Levinson Z, Hulver S, Neuman T. KFF: Hospital Charity Care: How It Works and Why It Matters. KFF website. November 3, 2022. https://www.kff.org/health-costs/issue-brief/hospital-charity-care-how-it-works-and-why-it-matters/

5. Wikipedia Federally Qualified Health Center. https://en.wikipedia.org/wiki/Federally_Qualified_Health_Center
6. Rural Health Information Hub. Rural Hospitals. RHI hub website. February 10, 2022. https://www.ruralhealthinfo.org/topics/hospitals#designations

Chapter 15

1. Moore H. Blount Memorial Hospital CEO Resigns After Months of Back and Forth with County Mayor. WATE.com. November 28, 2023. https://www.wate.com/news/top-stories/blount-memorial-ceo-resigns/
2. Franklin M. Blount Commission Clears Path for Blount Memorial Hospital Partner Search. The Daily Times. January 22, 2024. https://www.thedailytimes.com/news/blount-commission-clears-path-for-blount-memorial-hospital-partner-search/article_90fa9a1c-b978-11ee-91d5-47ecb59e7877.html
3. Staff Writers. Blount Memorial Hospital Could Face an Audit After County Leaders Passed Resolution on Thursday. WBIR.com September 20, 2023. https://www.wbir.com/article/news/local/blount-county-bmh-independent-audit/51-eddd7e93-e723-41da-9ce0-e44e8ea9c5ab

Chapter 16

1. Wikipedia. Libor. https://en.wikipedia.org/wiki/Libor
2. Wikipedia. National Commission for Quality Insurance. https://en.wikipedia.org/wiki/National_Committee_for_Quality_Assurance
3. Millenson M. Medicare, Fair Pay, and the AMA: The Forgotten History. *Health Affairs*. September 10, 2015. https://www.healthaffairs.org/content/forefront/medicare-fair-pay-and-ama-forgotten-history
4. Wikipedia. Herbert Haft. https://en.wikipedia.org/wiki/Herbert_Haft
5. Sullivan P. Discount Retailing Giant Stoked Bitter Family Feud. *The Washington Post*. September 3, 2004. https://www.washingtonpost.com/wp-dyn/articles/A56668-2004Sep2.html
6. Wikipedia. Robert Haft. https://en.wikipedia.org/wiki/Robert_Haft
7. Privia Health LLC. Privia Health Raises $12.3M from Healthcare Industry Insiders. Press Release. Privia Health. April 17, 2012. https://www.businesswire.com/news/home/20120417005410/en/Privia-Health-Raises-12.3M-from-Healthcare-Industry-Insiders
8. Staff Writers. Goldman Sachs Group Now Owns 21.70% of Privia Health Group (PRVA). Nasdaq.com website. February 14, 2023. https://www.nasdaq.com/articles/goldman-sachs-group-now-owns-21.70-of-privia-health-group-prva
9. Wikipedia. Bain Capital. https://en.wikipedia.org/wiki/Bain_Capital#
10. Wikipedia. Oscar Health. https://en.wikipedia.org/wiki/Oscar_Health
11. Madden B. The Rise and Fall of Envision Healthcare. Workweek.com. May 11, 2023. https://workweek.com/2023/05/11/the-rise-and-fall-of-envision-healthcare/

12. Pollitz K. No Surprises Act Implementation: What to Expect in 2022. KFF.com website. December 10, 2021. https://www.kff.org/affordable-care-act/issue-brief/no-surprises-act-implementation-what-to-expect-in-2022/
13. Knauth D. Bankrupt Envision Healthcare Approved to Split in Two, Cut Debt. Reuters. October 11, 2023. https://www.reuters.com/business/healthcare-pharmaceuticals/bankrupt-envision-healthcare-gets-ok-split-two-cut-7-bln-debt-2023-10-11/
14. Wikipedia. Silicon Valley Bank. https://en.wikipedia.org/wiki/Silicon_Valley_Bank
15. Wikipedia. Collapse of Silicon Valley Bank. https://en.wikipedia.org/wiki/Collapse_of_Silicon_Valley_Bank
16. Tuner B. Digital Health Could Get a Reset Following Silicon Valley Bank Failure. *Modern Healthcare*. March 10, 2023. https://www.modernhealthcare.com/finance/silicon-valley-bank-failure-digital-health-investments-fdic
17. Joyner A. More Than 110 VC Firms, Led by General Catalyst, Are Banding Together in Support of Silicon Valley Bank. Business Insider. March 11, 2023. https://www.businessinsider.com/silicon-valley-bank-general-catalyst-vc-firms-support-statement-2023-3

Chapter 17

1. Summa Health and General Catalyst's HATCo Announce Plans for Acquisition That Will Transform the Future of Healthcare. Business Wire. January 17, 2024. https://www.businesswire.com/news/home/20240117664403/en/Summa-Health-and-General-Catalyst%E2%80%99s-HATCo-announce-plans-for-acquisition-that-will-transform-the-future-of-healthcare
2. Taneja H, Harrison M. The Future of Health: A Bold Leap Forward. General Catalyst website. October 8, 2023. https://www.generalcatalyst.com/perspectives/the-future-of-health
3. Brodwin E. Venture Capital Firm General Catalyst to Buy Ohio Health System Summa Health. Axios. January 17, 2024. https://www.axios.com/2024/01/17/summa-health-ohio-general-catalyst
4. Wikipedia. Optum. https://en.wikipedia.org/wiki/Optum
5. Weber S. 10% of US Physicians Work for or Under UnitedHealth. Is That a Problem? Medscape. December 14, 2023. https://www.medscape.com/viewarticle/10-us-physicians-work-or-under-unitedhealth-problem-2023a1000vhg
6. UnitedHealth's Optum Revenues Surpass $100B for 1st Time. Becker's. January 15, 2019. https://www.beckerspayer.com/payer/unitedhealth-s-optum-revenues-surpass-100b-for-1st-time.html
7. Japsen B. Optum To Provide More Than Half of UnitedHealth's 2020 Profits. *Forbes*. December 3, 2019. https://www.forbes.com/sites/brucejapsen/2019/12/03/optum-to-provide-more-than-half-of-unitedhealths-2020-profits/?sh=4da231a49598

ADDITIONAL RECOMMENDED READINGS

For a basic summary of healthcare economics, read this brief but highly useful article:

The Basics of Healthcare Economics, Finance, and Budgeting for the New Physician by Timothy N. Liesching. *Physician Leadership Journal.* November 8, 2021. https://www.physicianleaders.org/articles/basics-healthcare-economics-finance-budgeting-new-physician-leader

For a clear summary of the basis of health insurance, read this excellent handbook:

Insurance Handbook. Insurance Information Institute. 2010. https://www.iii.org/publications/insurance-handbook/regulatory-and-financial-environment/reinsurance

For an overview of CMS value-based payment models, read the introduction to this report:

Accounting for Social Risk Factors in Medicare Payment: Identifying Social Risk Factors. National Academies of Sciences, Engineering, and Medicine. 2016. Washington, DC: The National Academies Press; 2016. https://doi.org/10.17226/21858.

For more information about CMS innovations regarding payment, read: https://www.cms.gov/priorities/innovation/models#views=models

For an excellent review of physician employment contracting inside and outside hospitals, especially how to incorporate non-FFS payments (e.g., PCMH, CIN, ACO, APMs, MSSP, and BPCI) into contracting, read:

Physician-Hospital Alignment and Compensation Models: The Second Generation by Max Reiboldt, Justin Chamblee, and Ellis "Mac" Knight. Washington, DC: American Association for Physician Leadership. 2017.

Read much more about "corporate medicine" in a landmark book by two Pulitzer Prize-winning investigative journalists here:

Critical Condition: How Health Care in America Became Big Business & Bad Medicine by Donald Barlett and James Steele. New York: Random House; 2005.

For more information on RBRVs/RVUs:

Development of the Resource-Based Relative Value Scale https://www.ama-assn.org/system/files/development-of-the-resource-based-relative-value-scale.pdf

For more information on Stark Laws:

Stark Regulation: A Historical and Current Review of the Self-Referral Laws by M. Kolber. *HEC Forum.* 2006;18(1):61–84.

For more information on financial implications of hospital readmissions:

Does a Reduction in Readmissions Result in Net Savings for Most Hospitals? An Examination of Medicare's Hospital Readmissions Reduction Program by O Yakusheva and GJ Hoffman. *Med Care Res Rev.* 2020;77(4):334–344.

For more on the co-dependent relationships of small community/regional hospitals and community prosperity:

The Hospital: Life, Death, and Dollars in a Small American Town by Brian Alexander. New York: St. Martin's Press; 2021.

For more on the role of quality improvements that were accounted in the numerator, and other various elements of the MLR management, read an excellent post and its accompanying links:

The Medical Loss Ratio's Mixed Record by Shelby Livingston. *Modern Healthcare.* March 14, 2020. https://www.modernhealthcare.com/insurance/medical-loss-ratios-mixed-record

Printed in the USA
CPSIA information can be obtained
at www.ICGtesting.com
CBHW051730150824
13220CB00003B/8

9 781960 762238